FOR DAELU

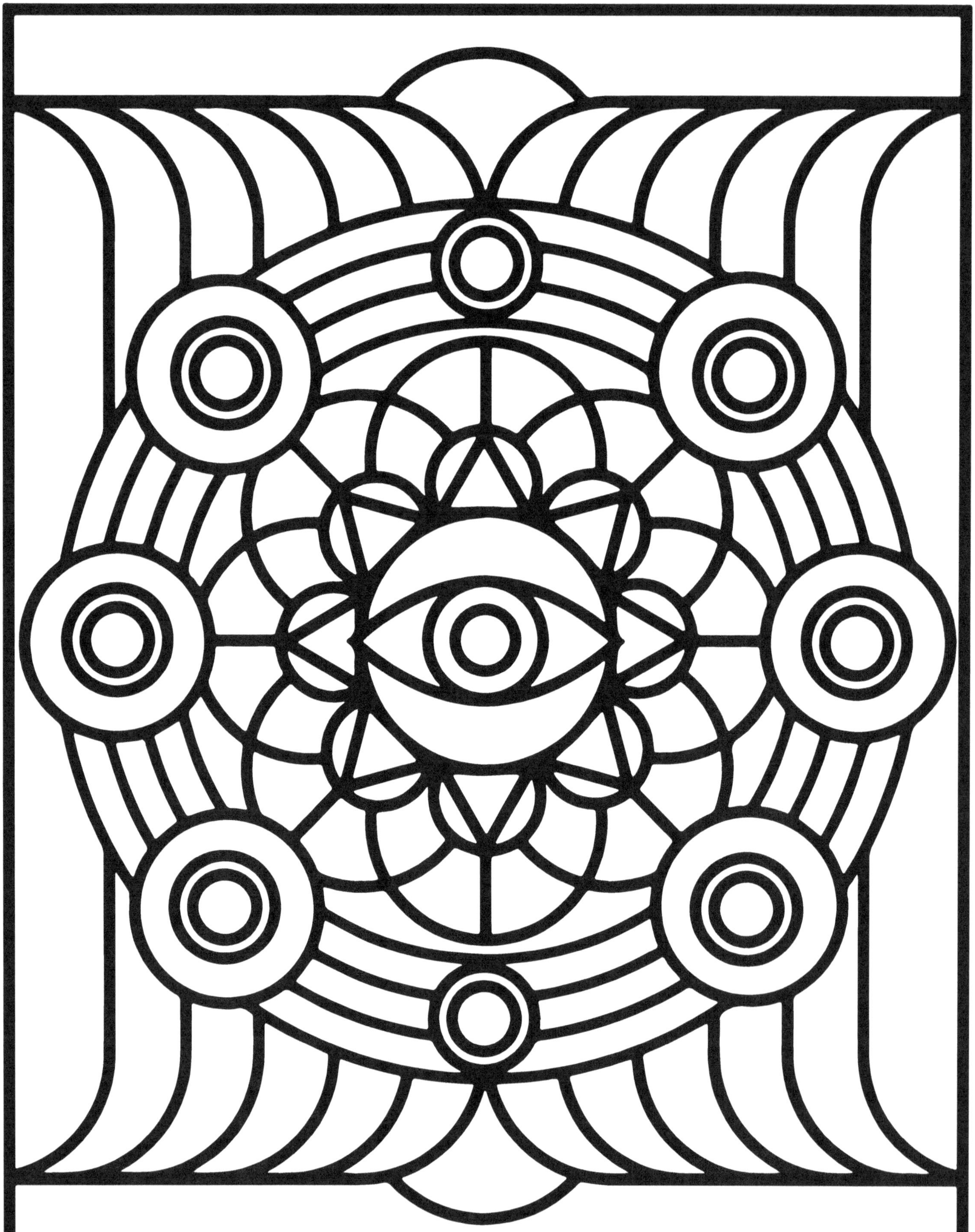

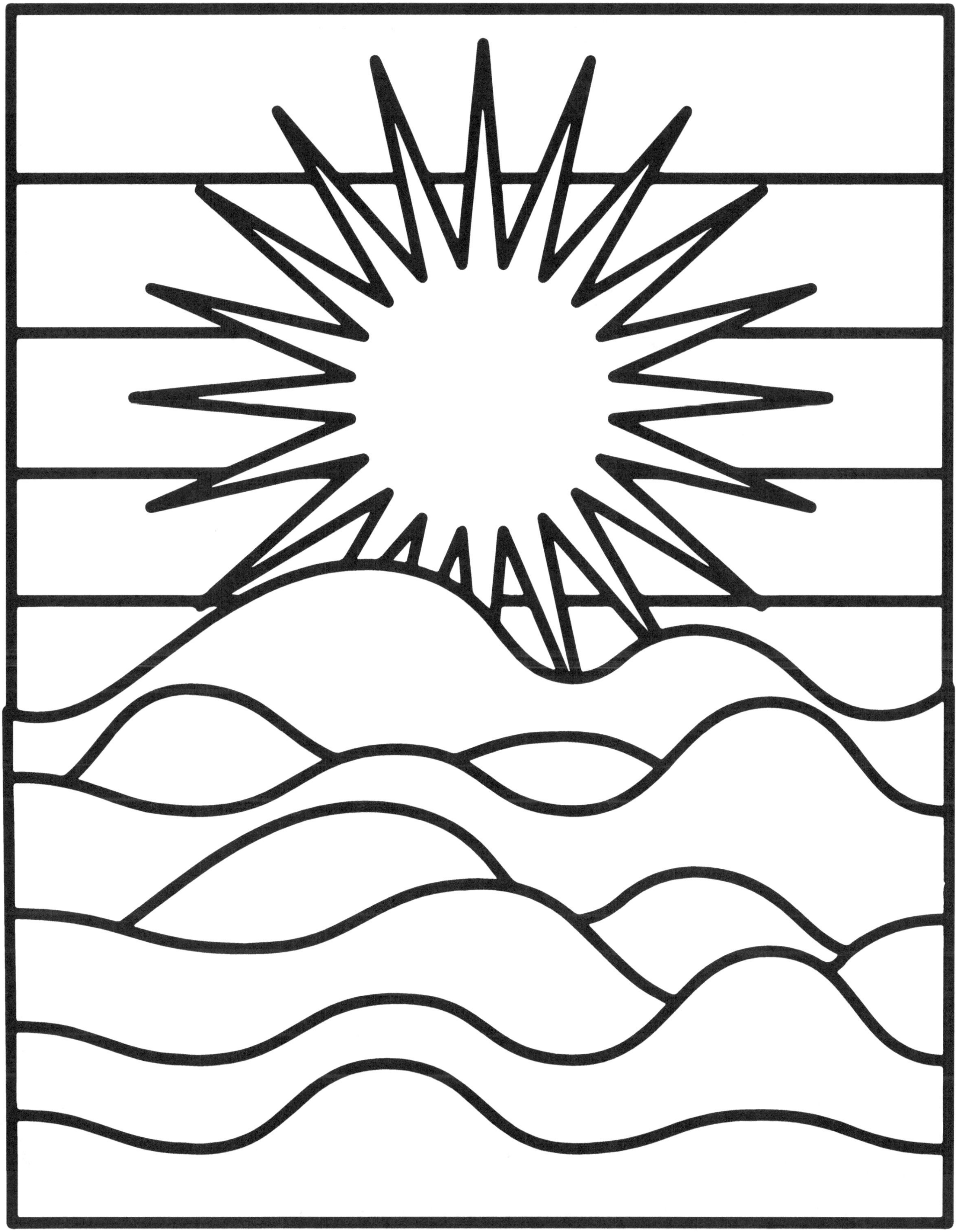

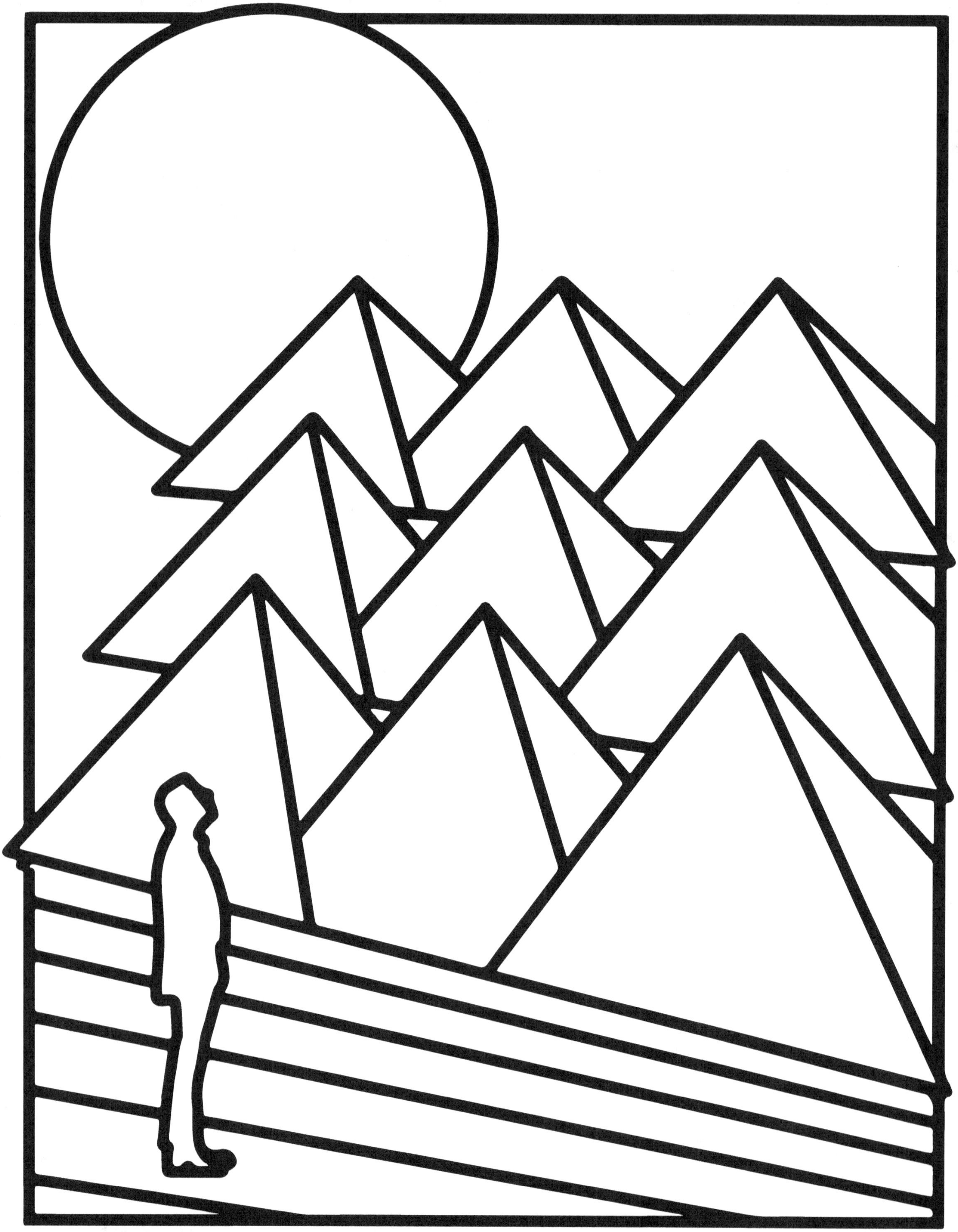

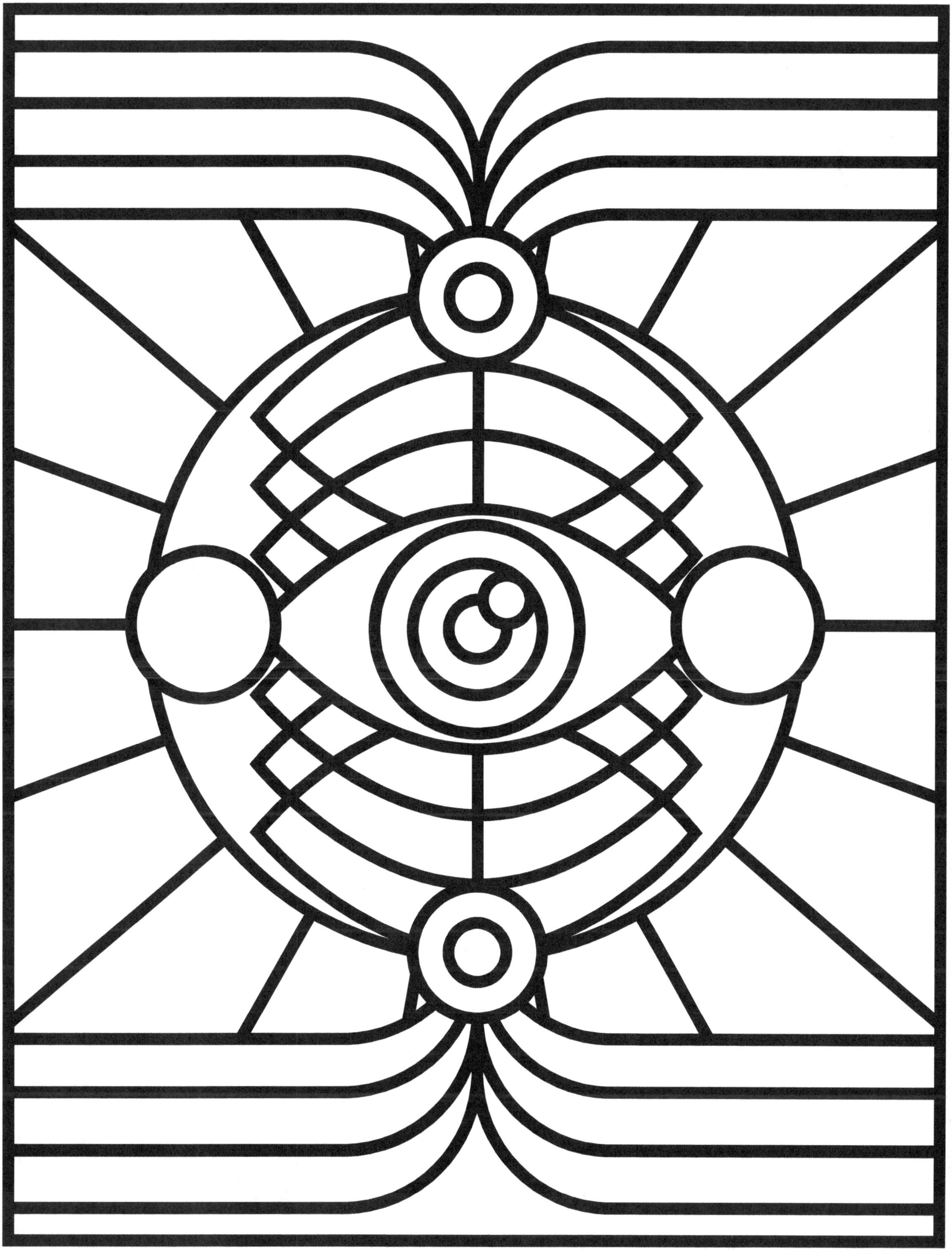

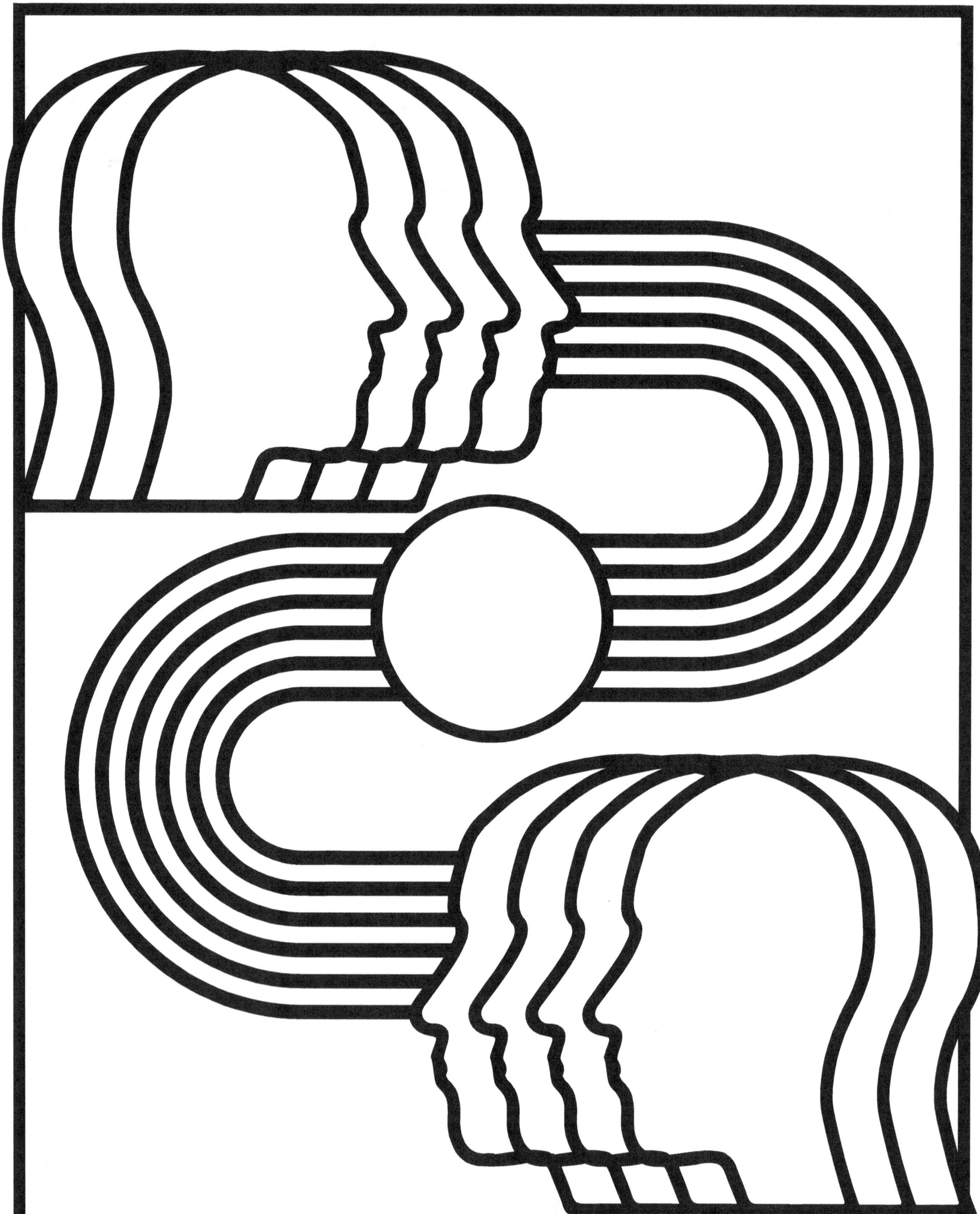

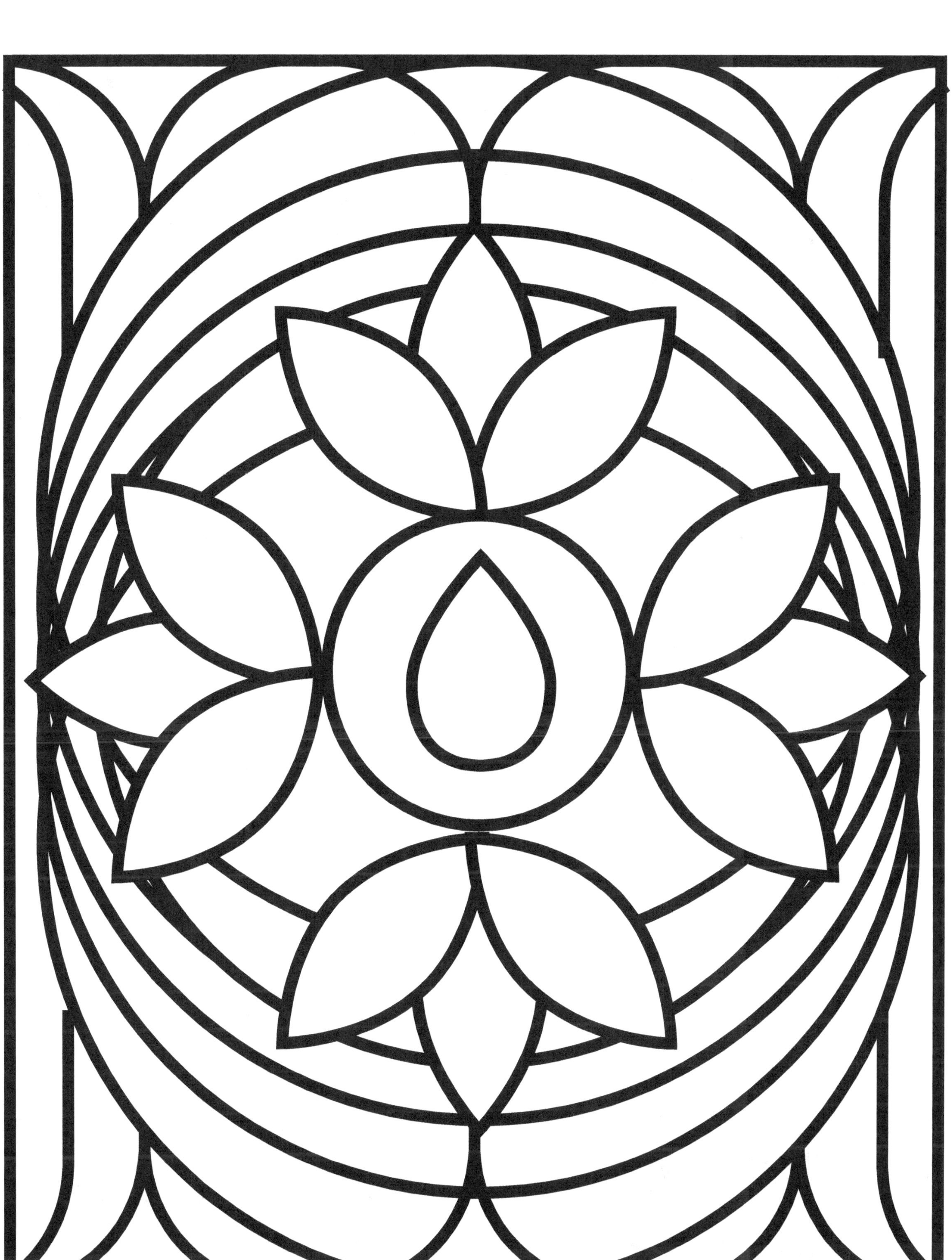

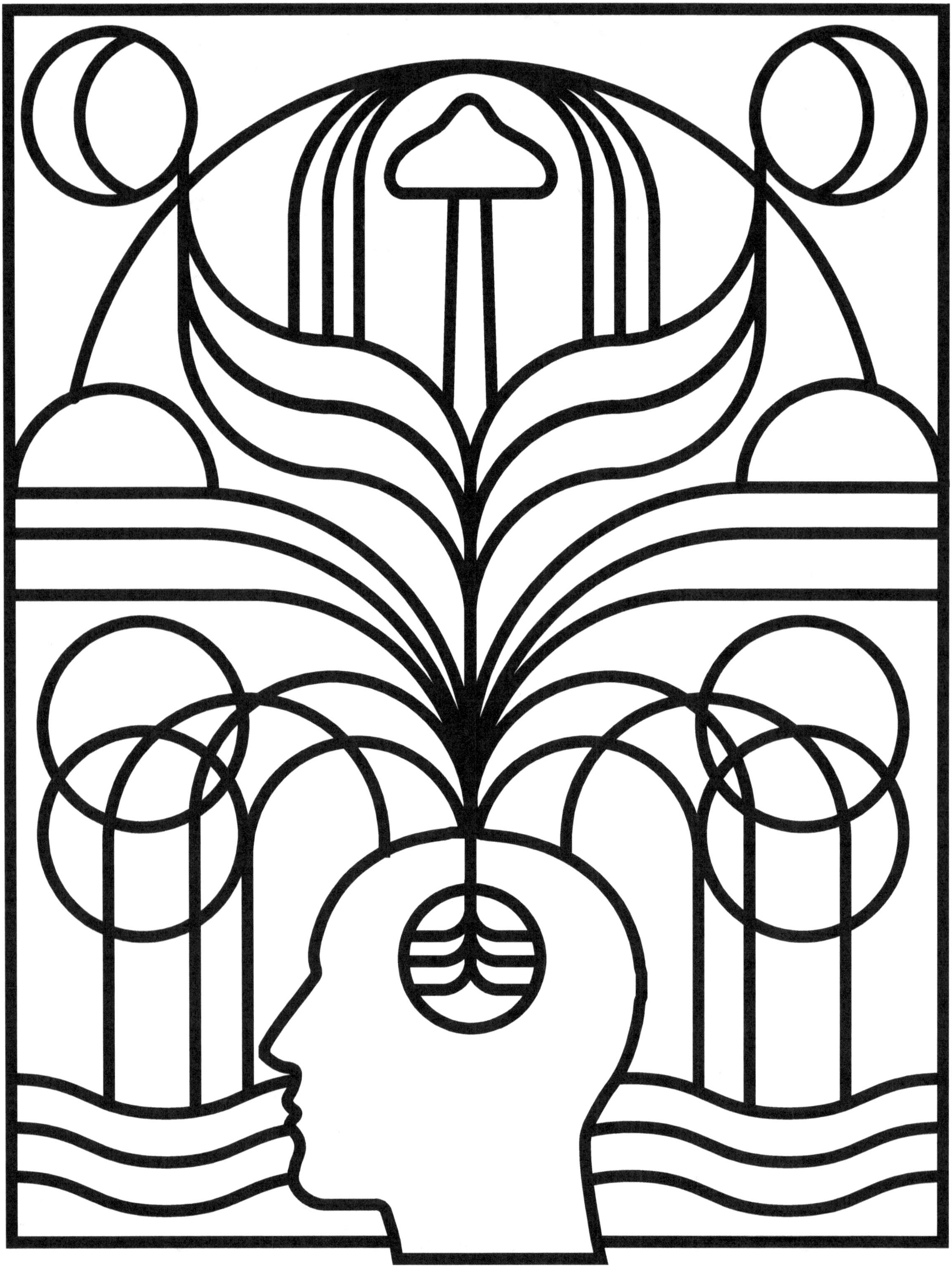

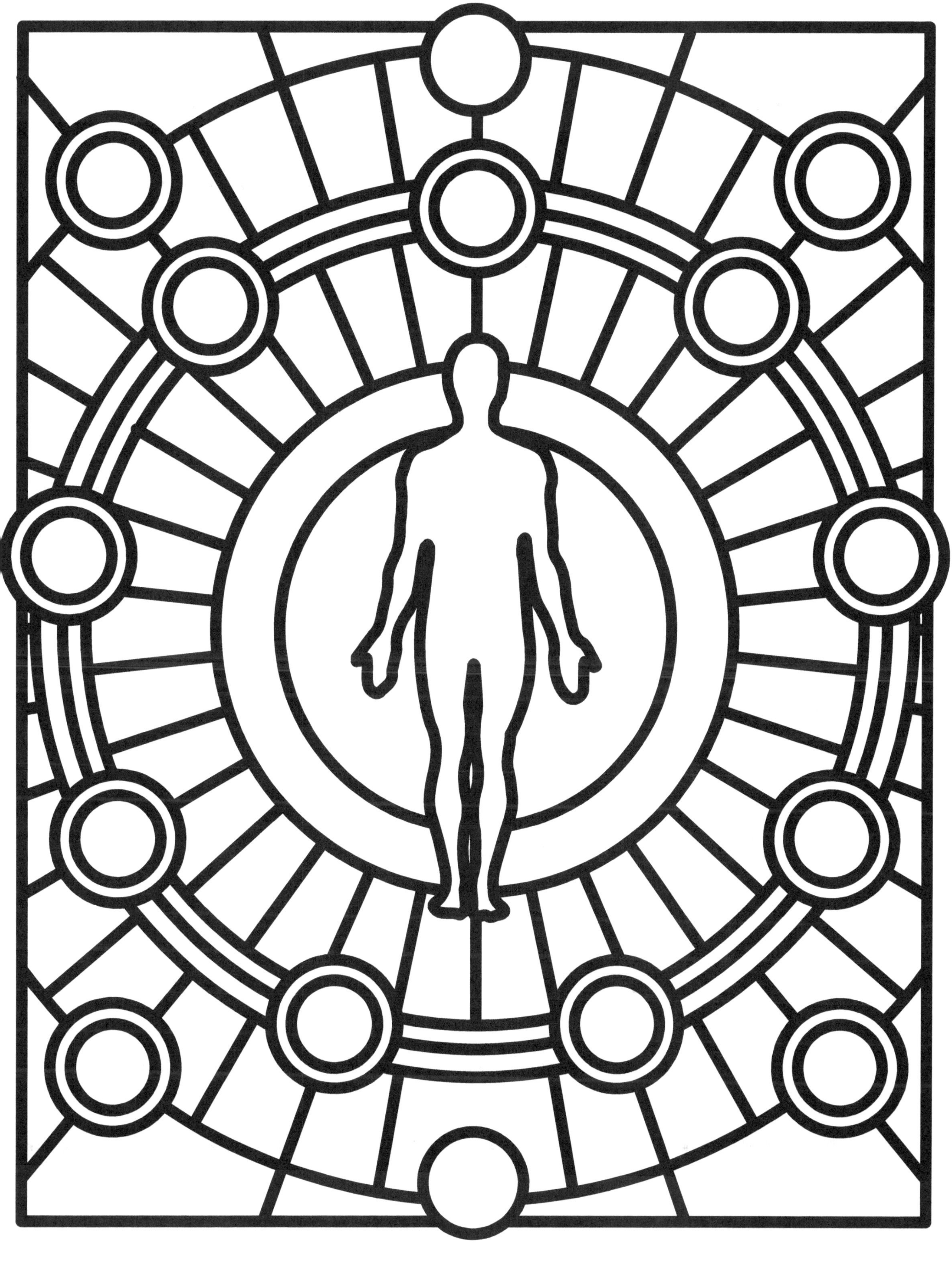

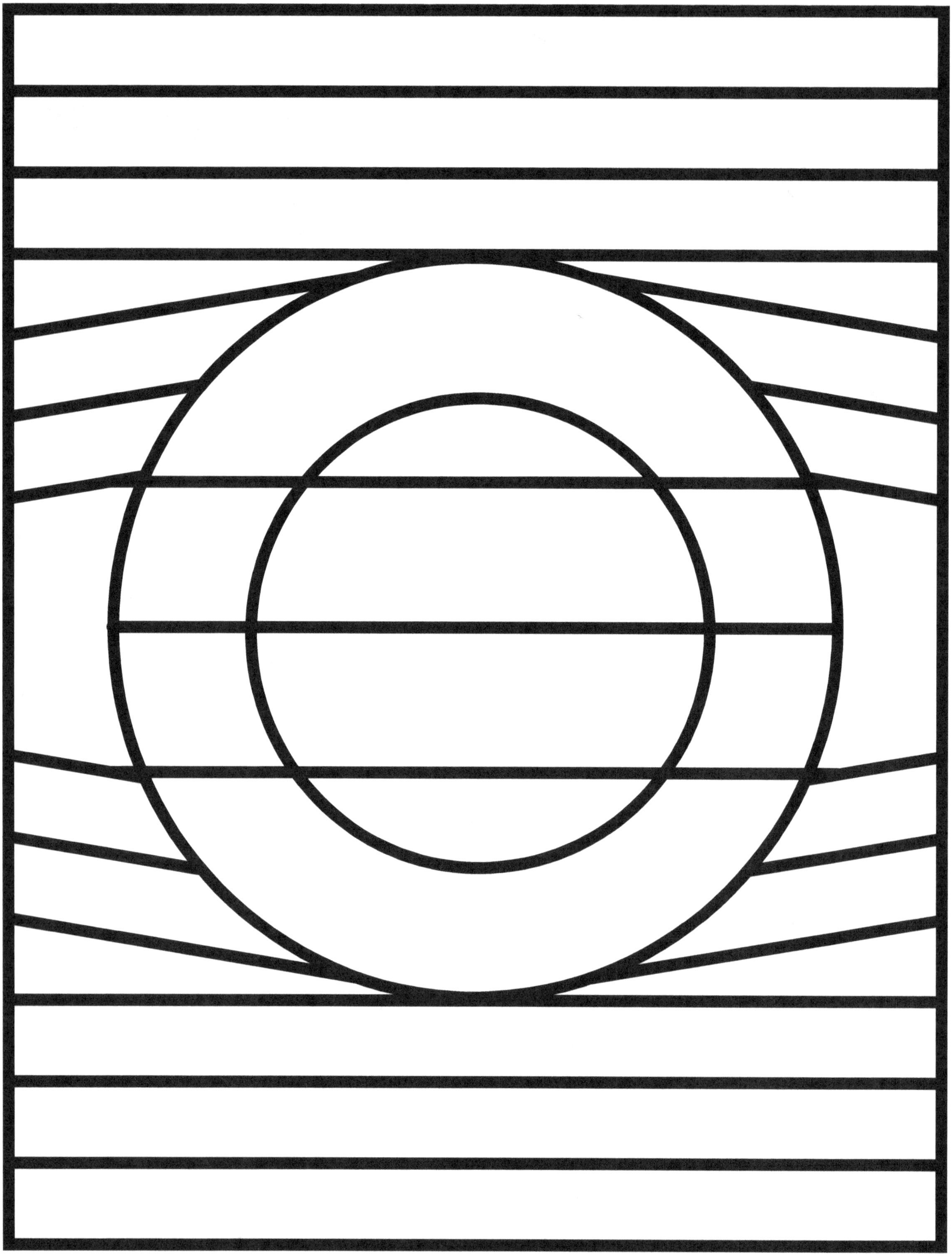

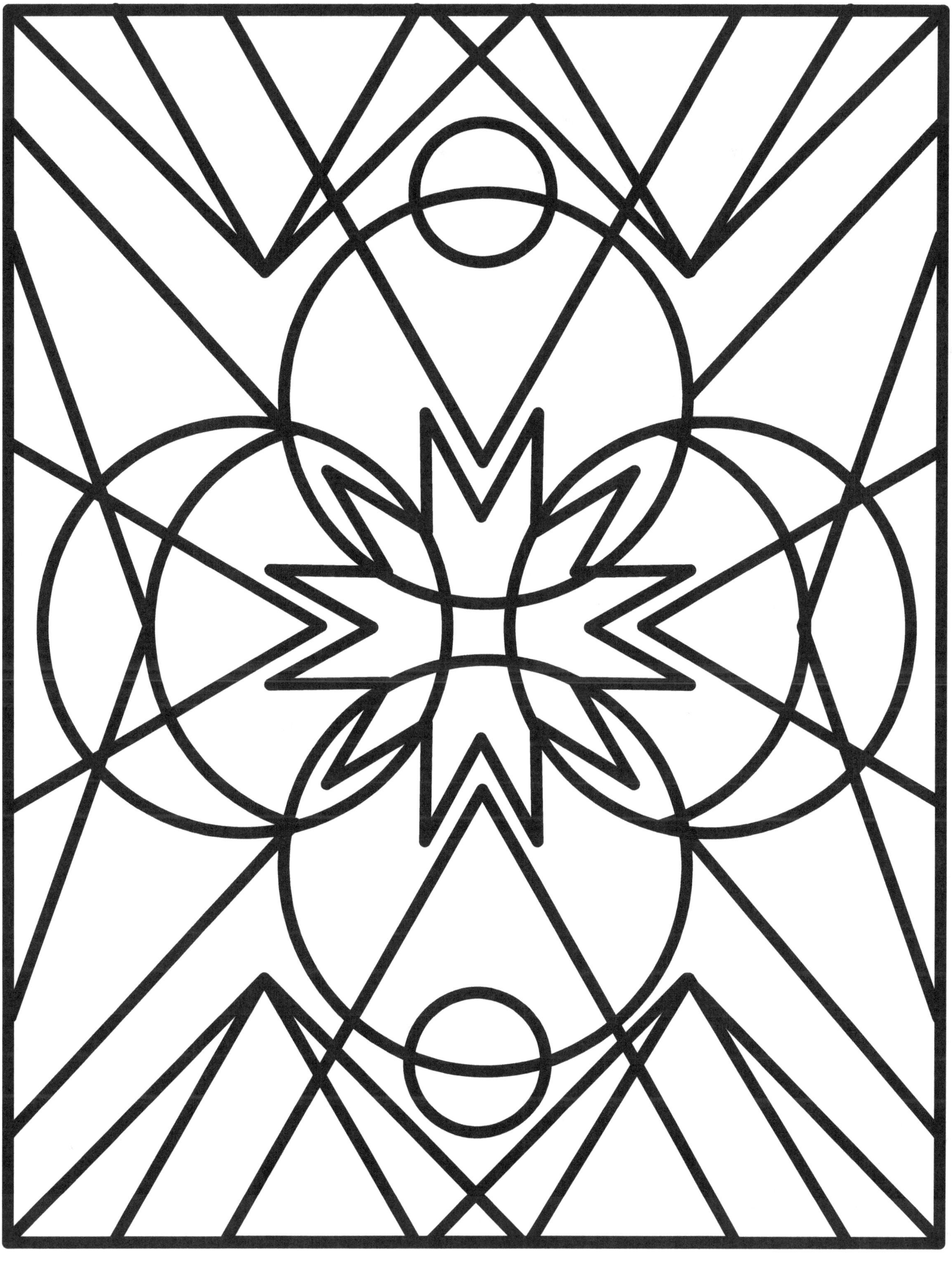

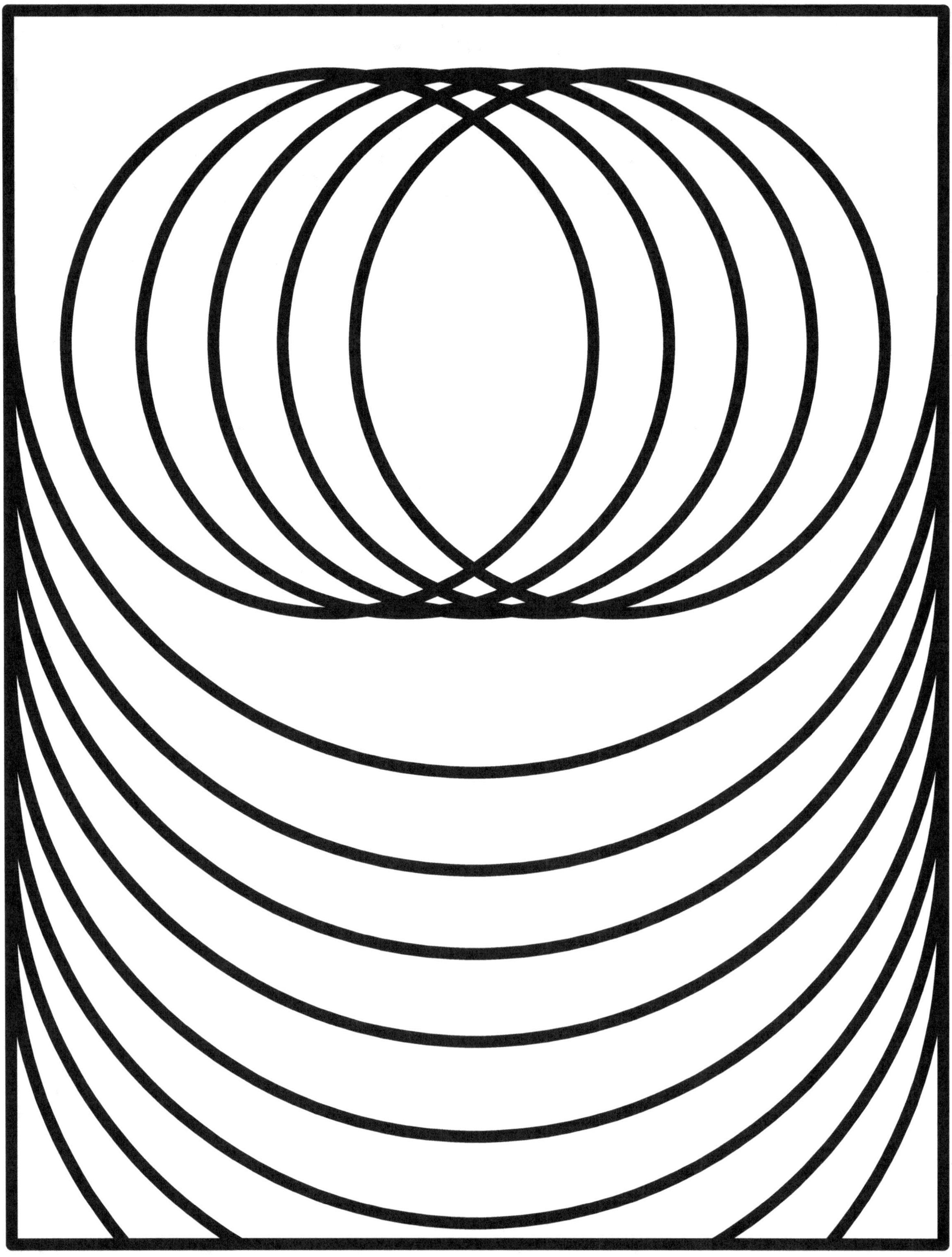

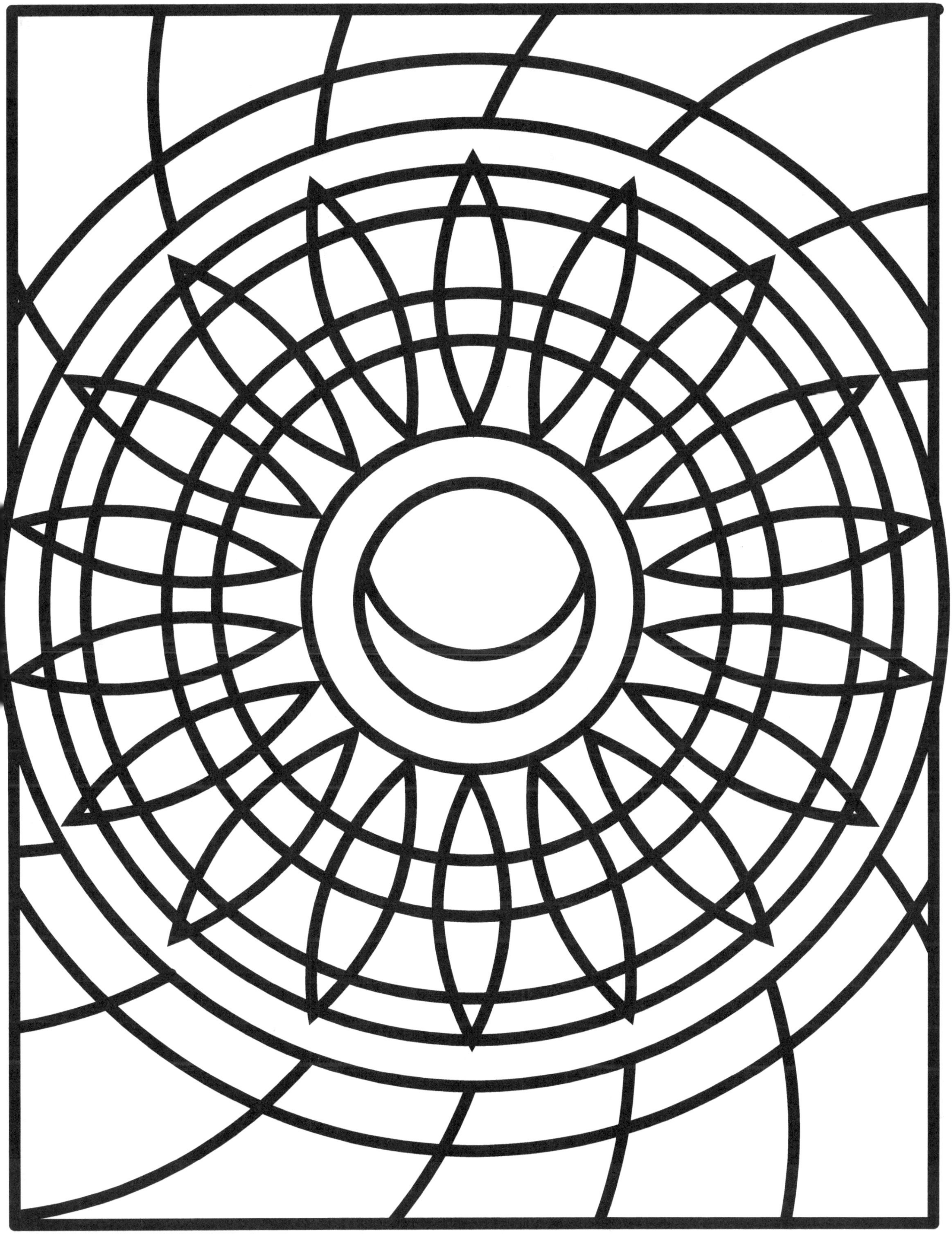

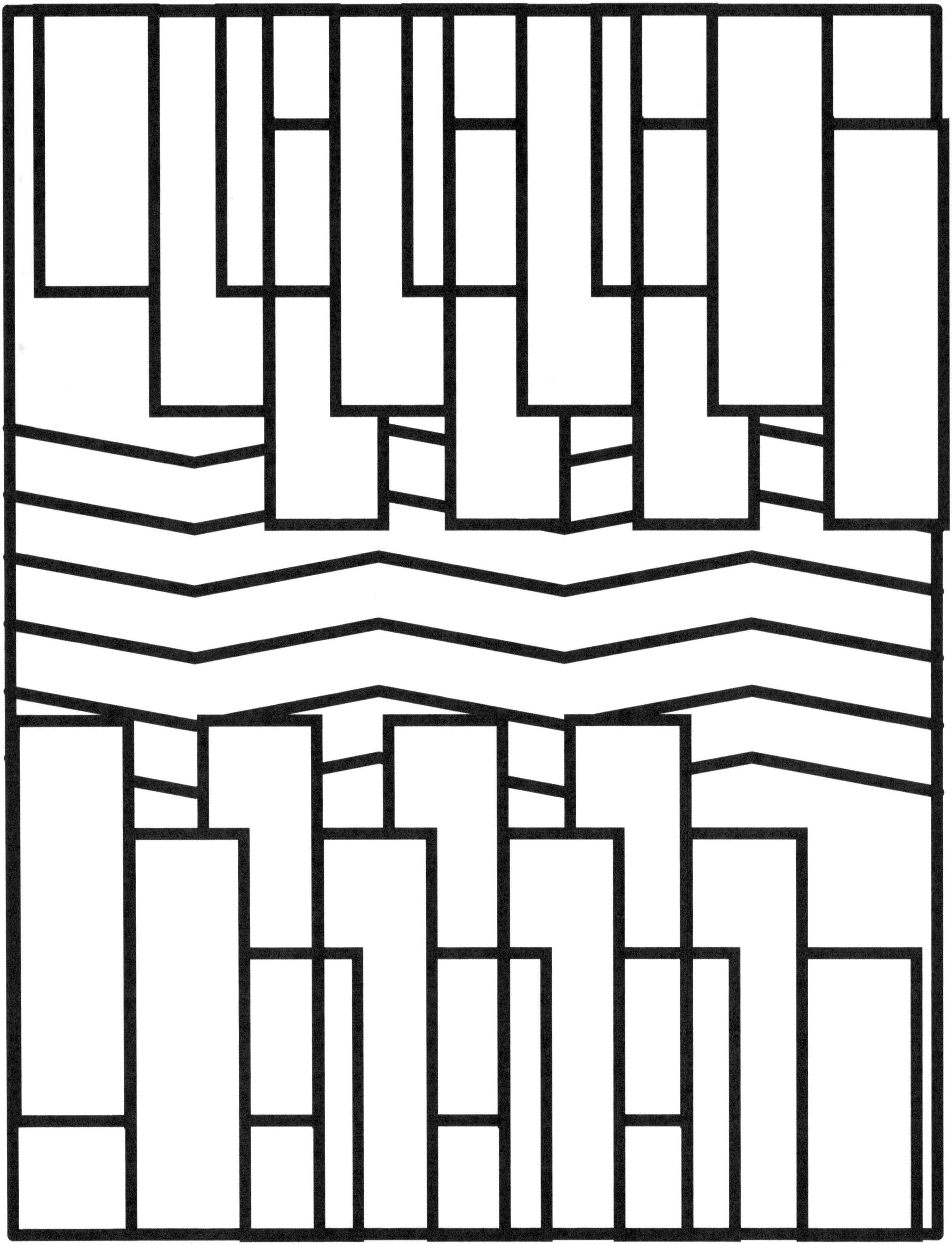

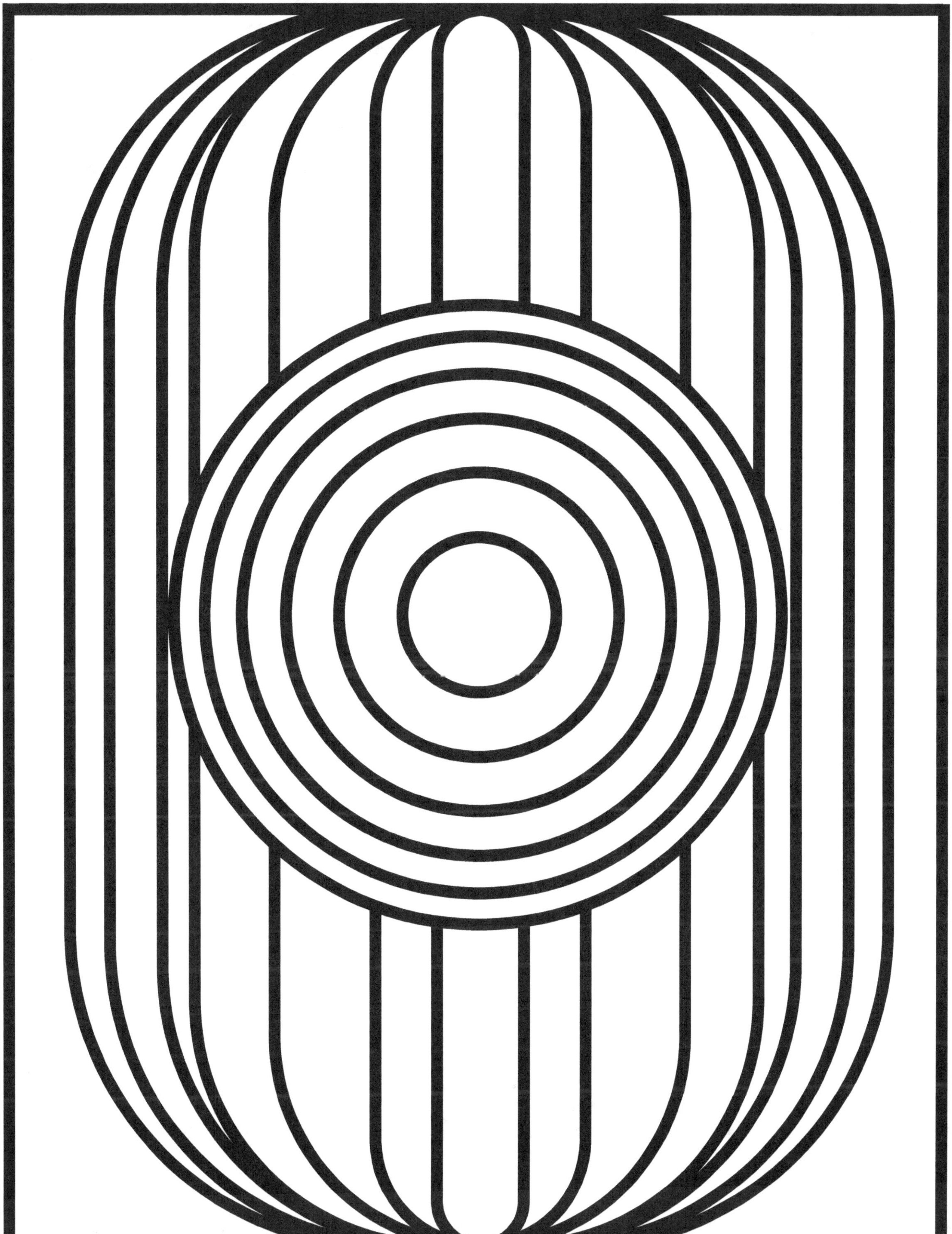

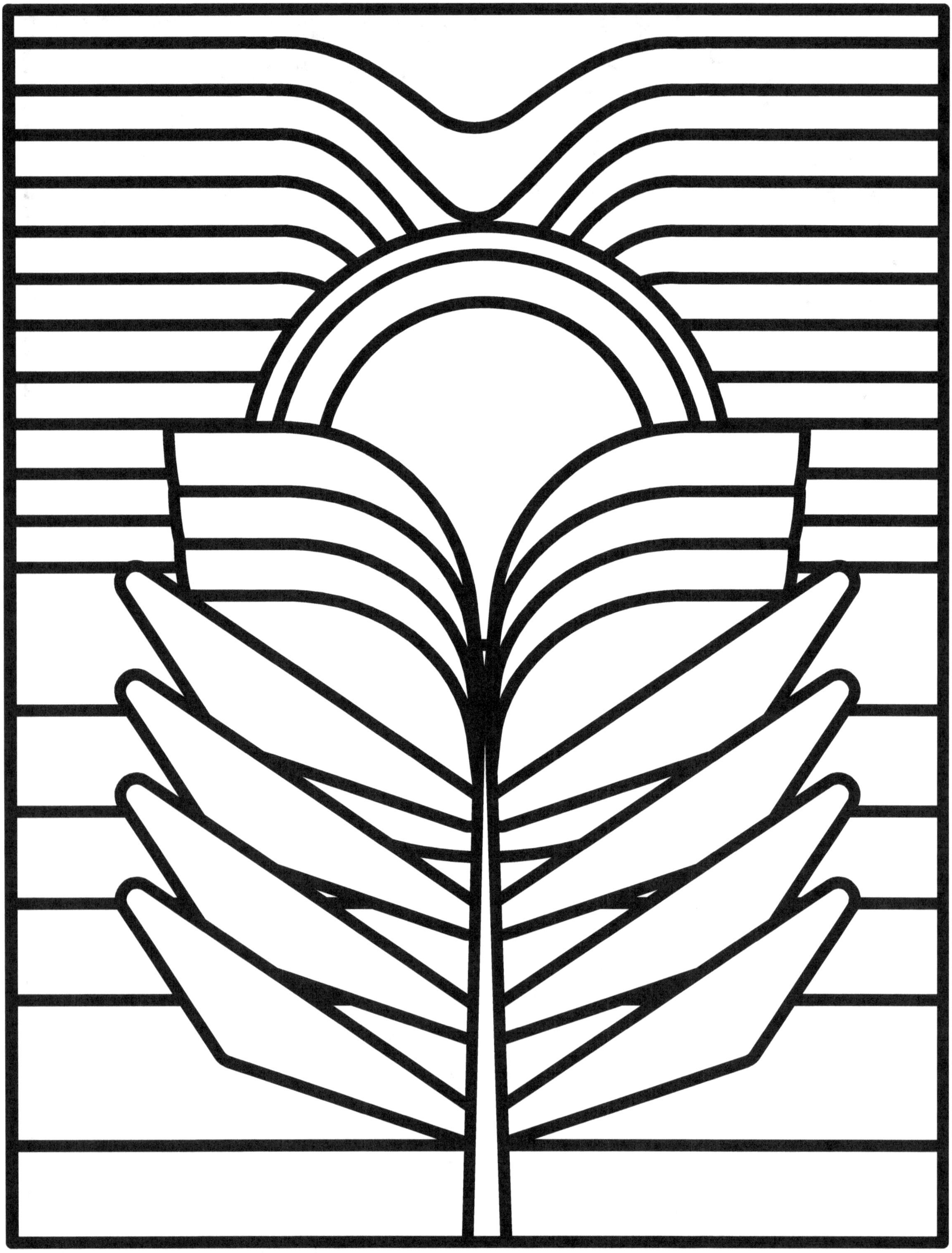

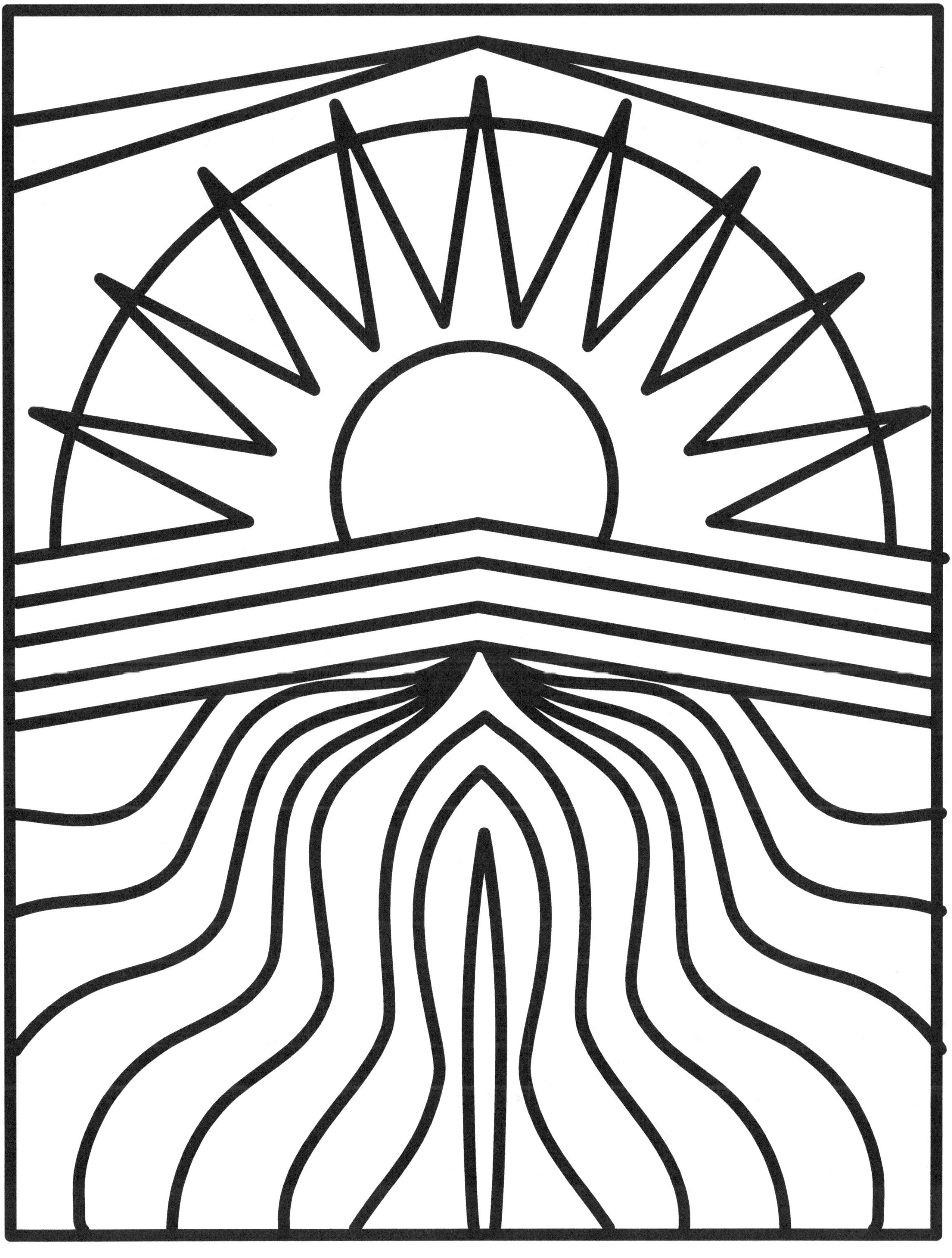

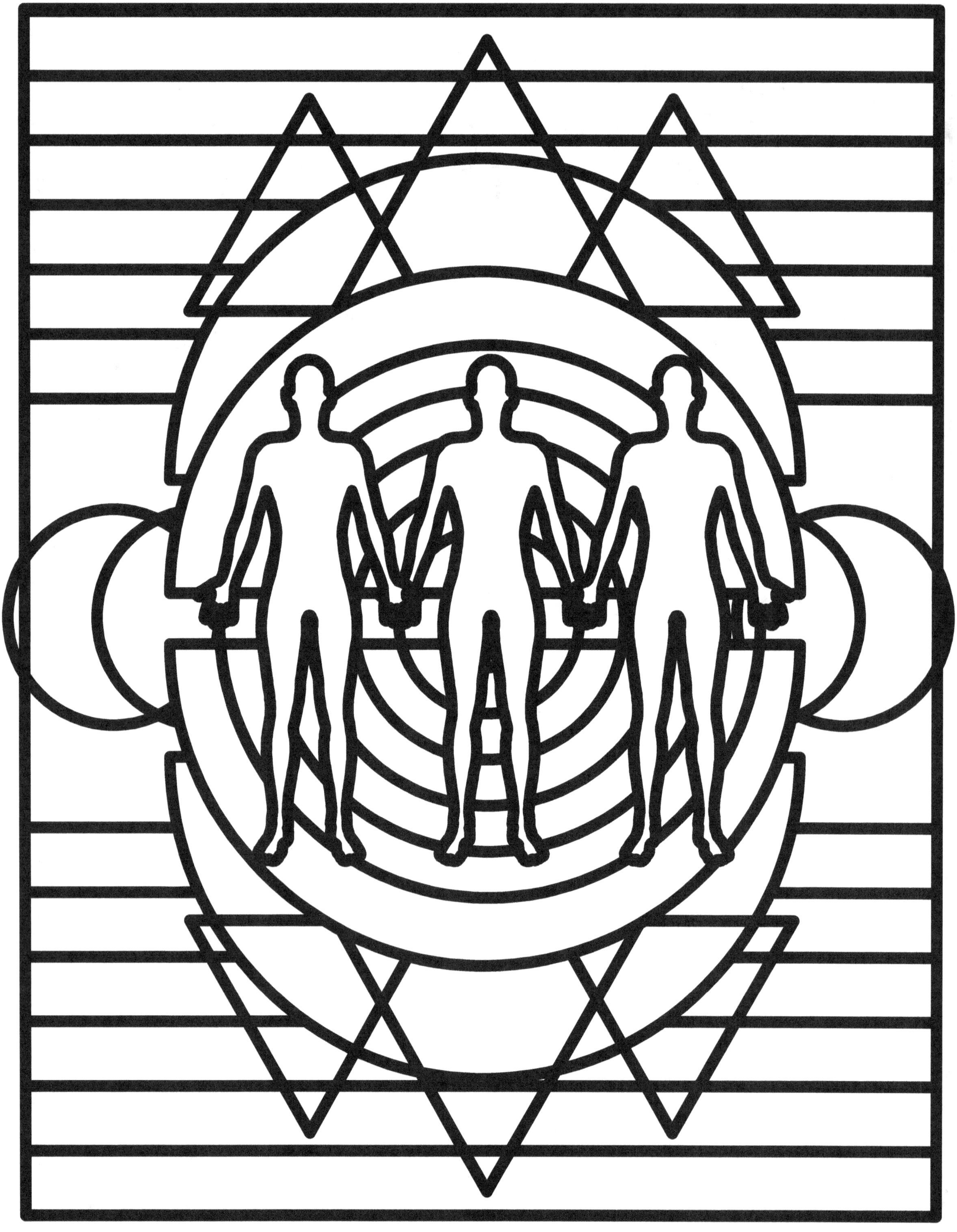

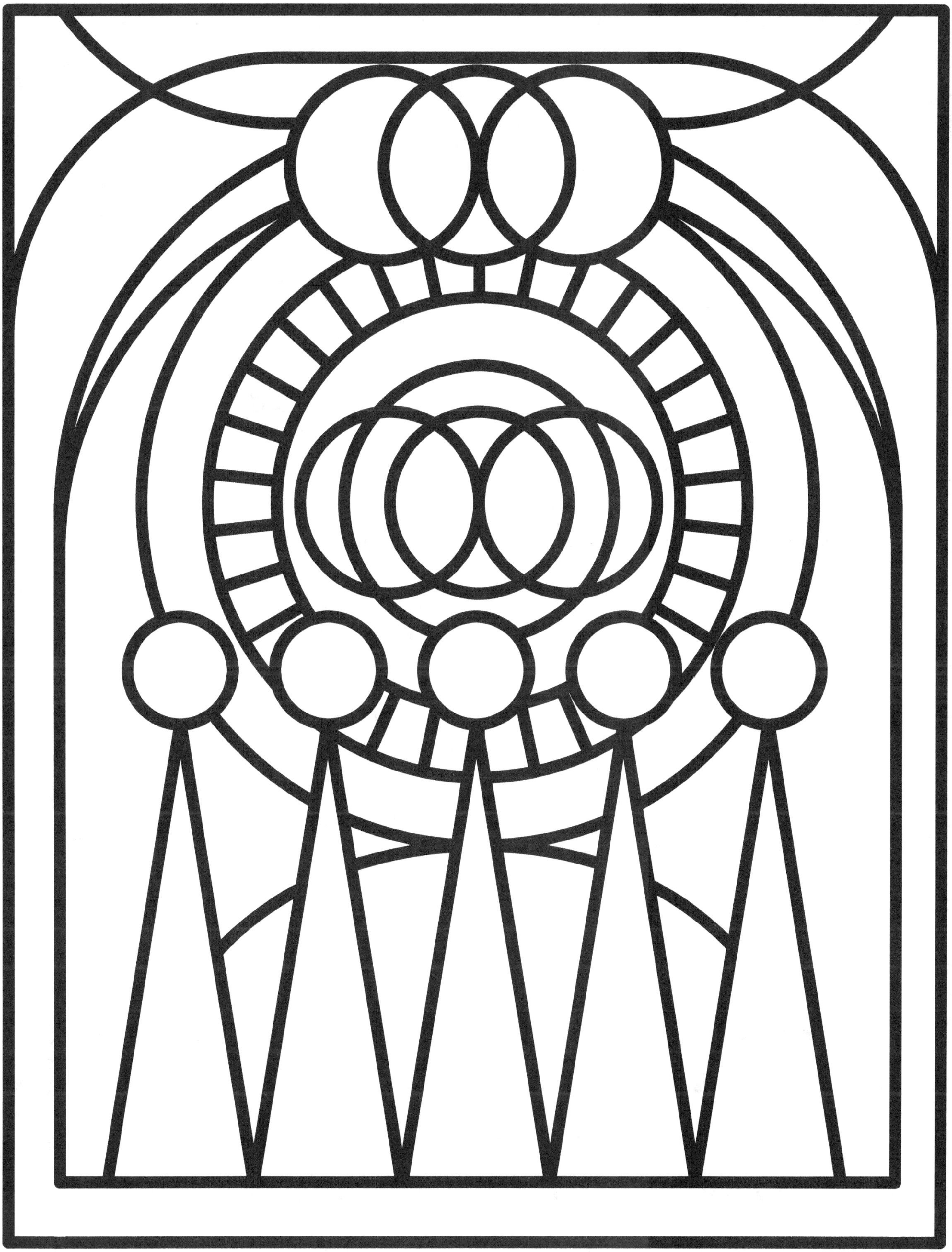

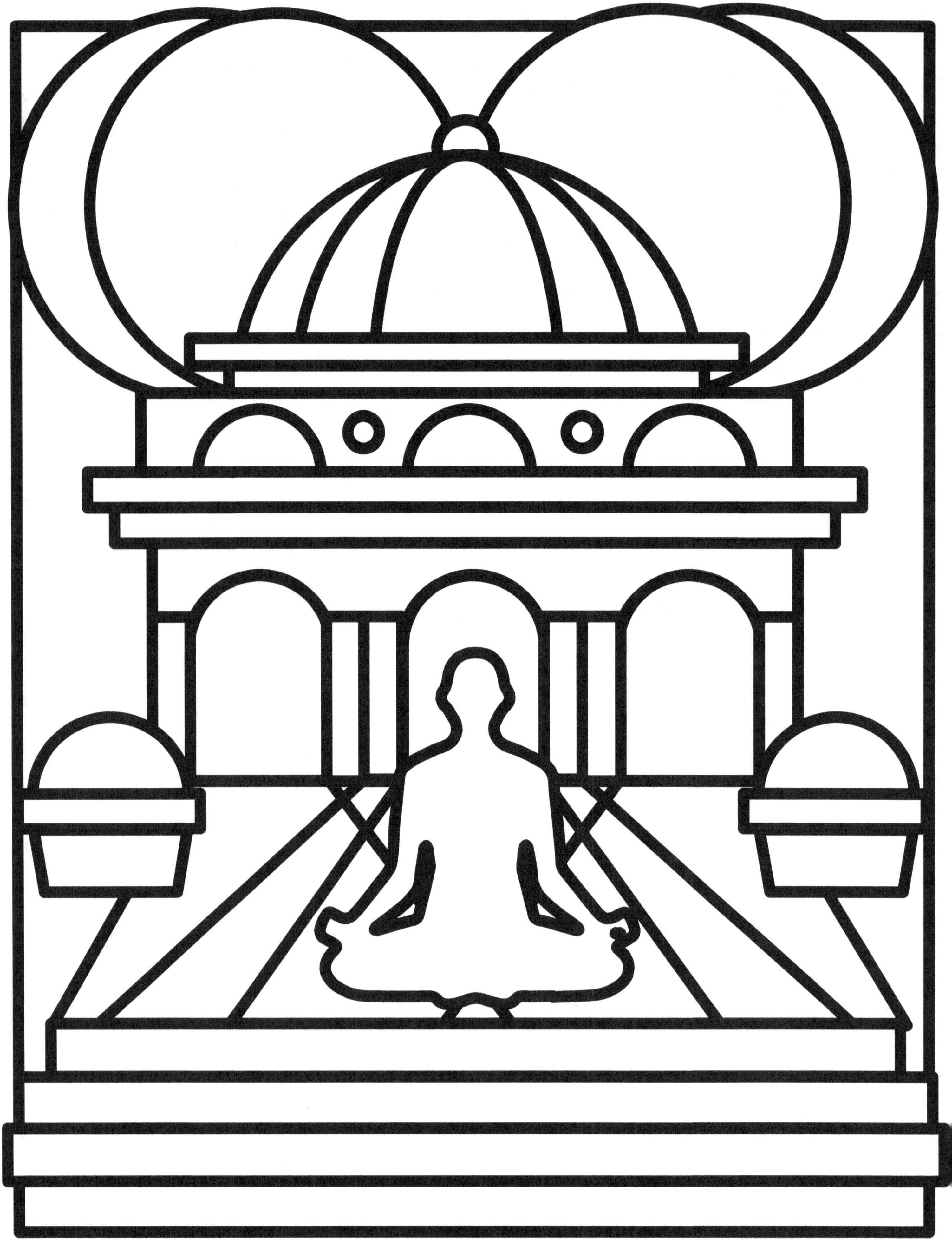

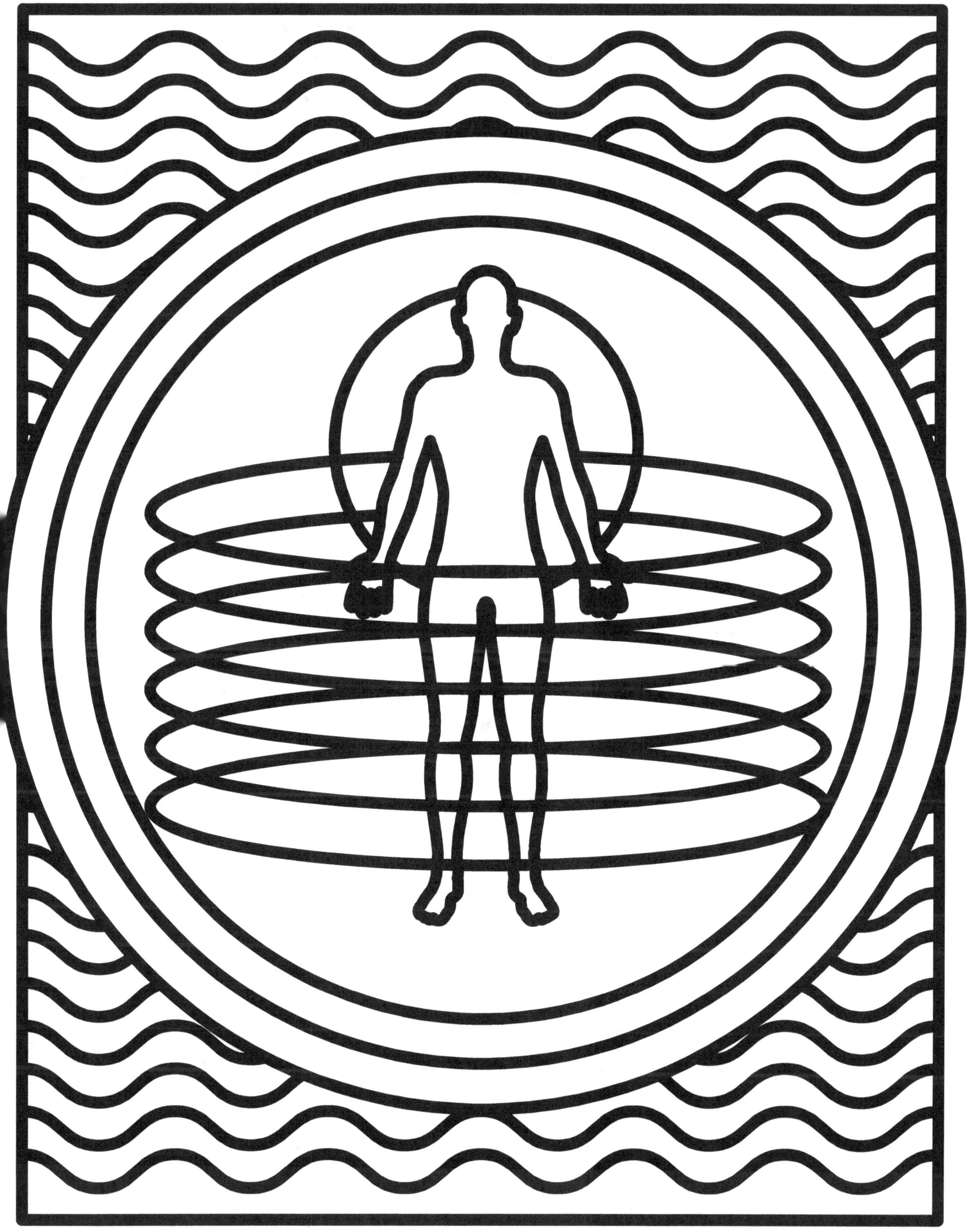

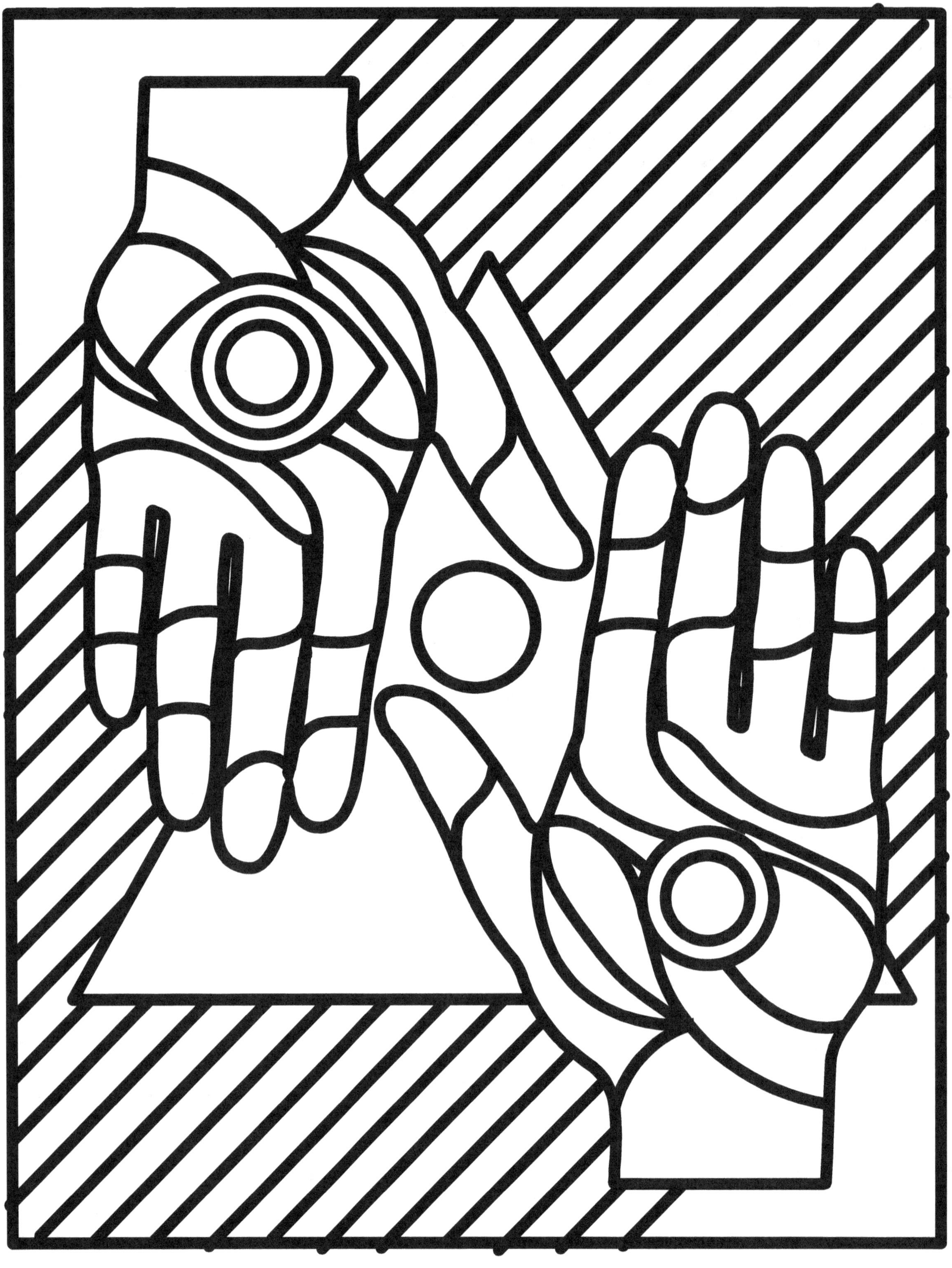

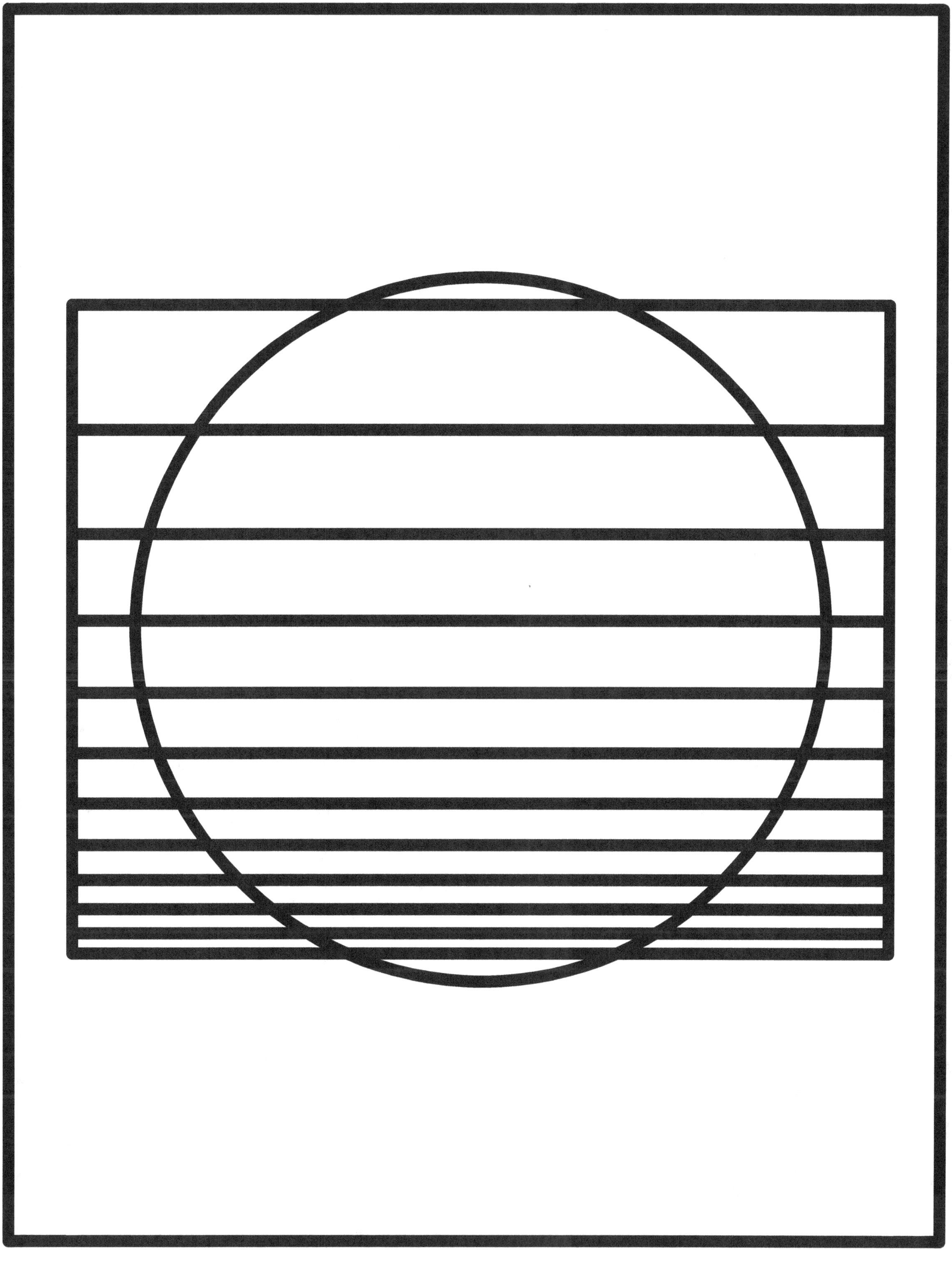

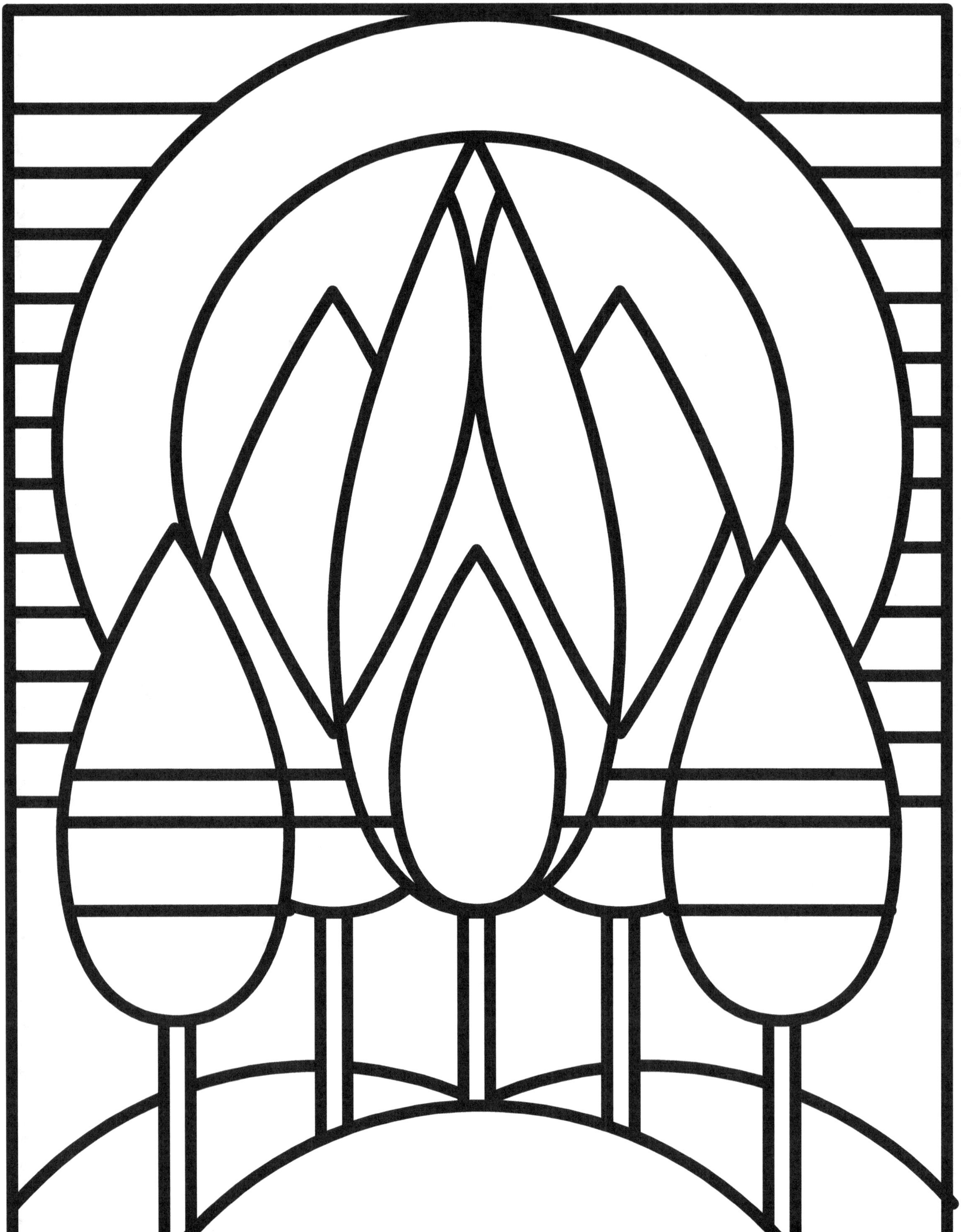

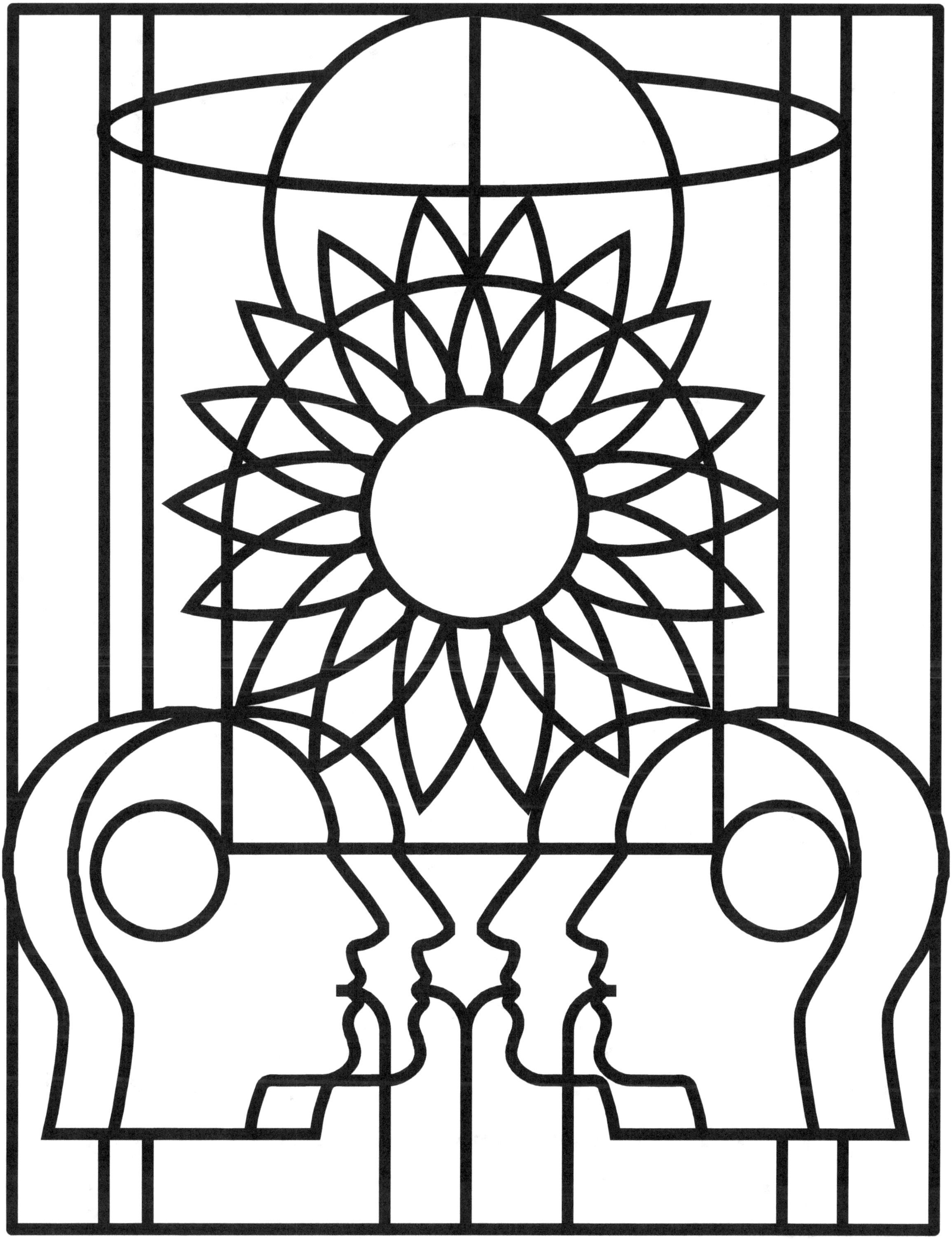

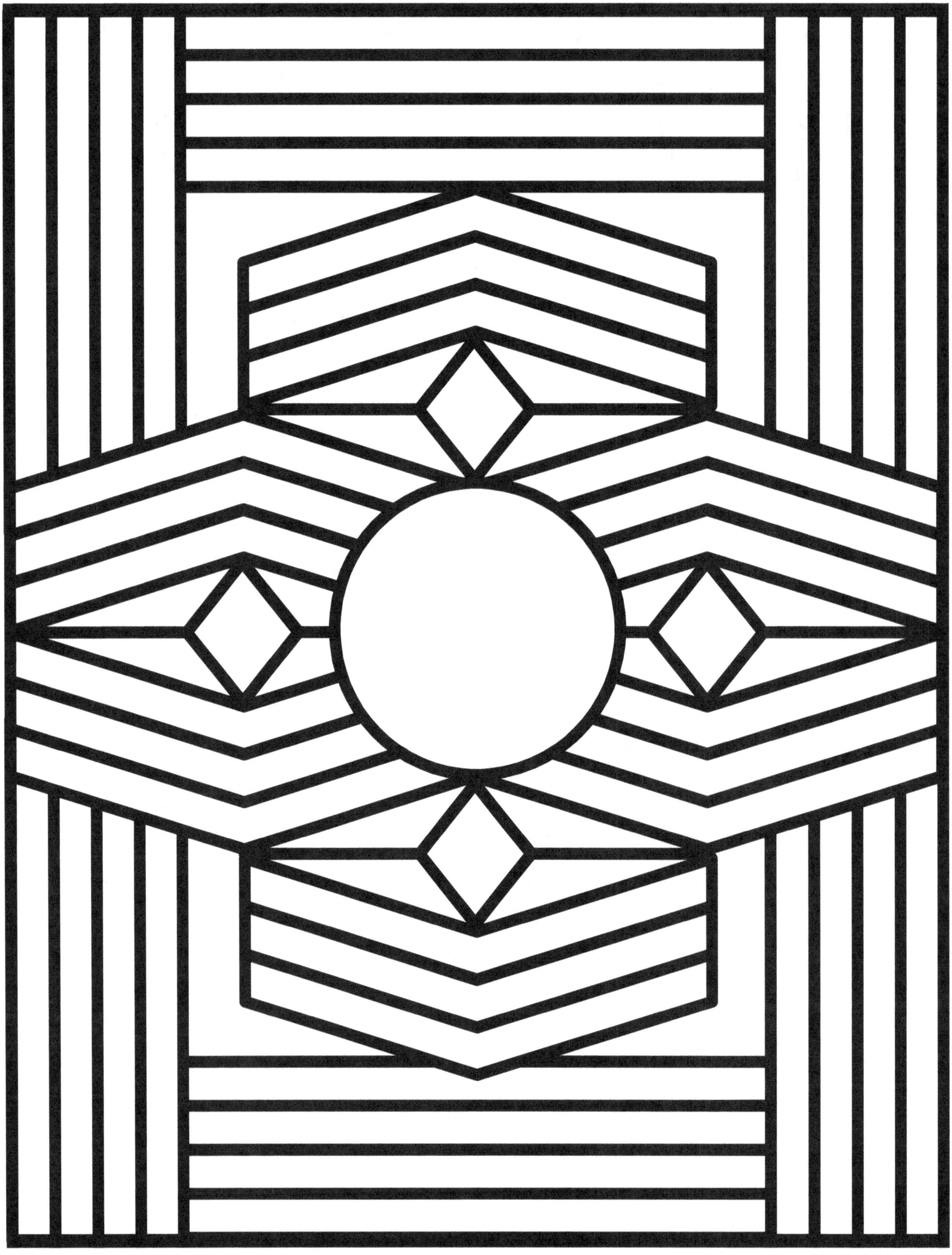

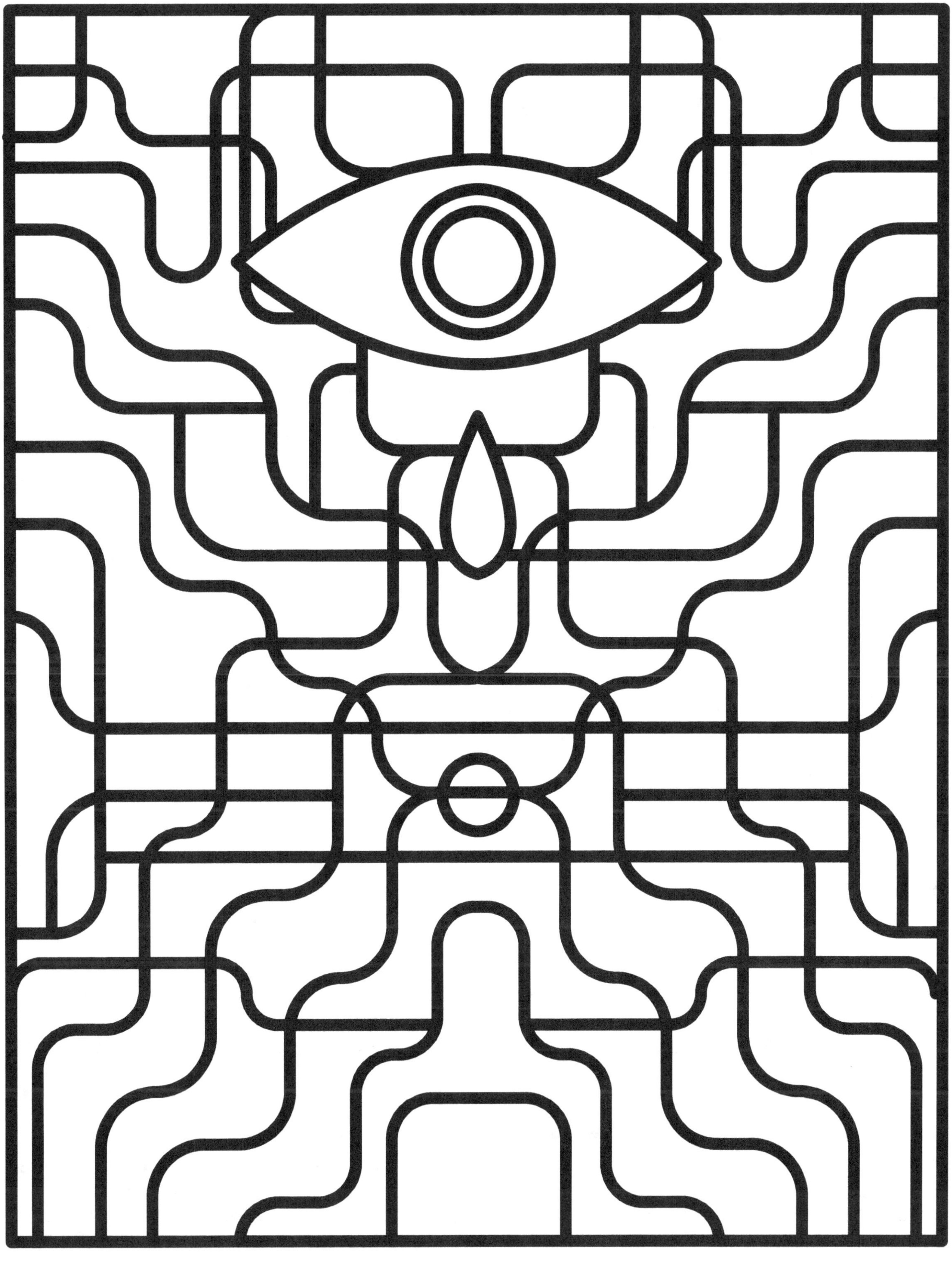

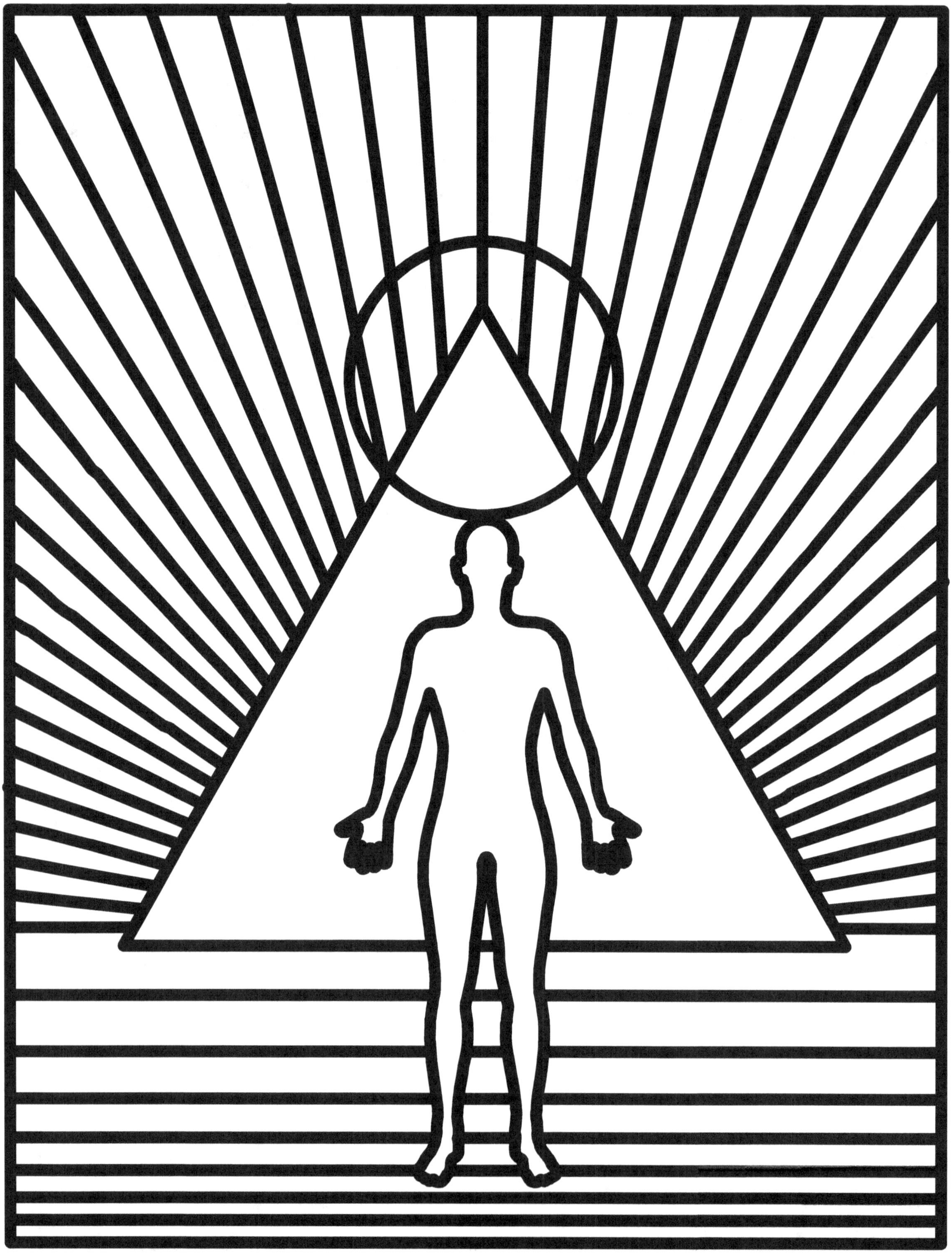

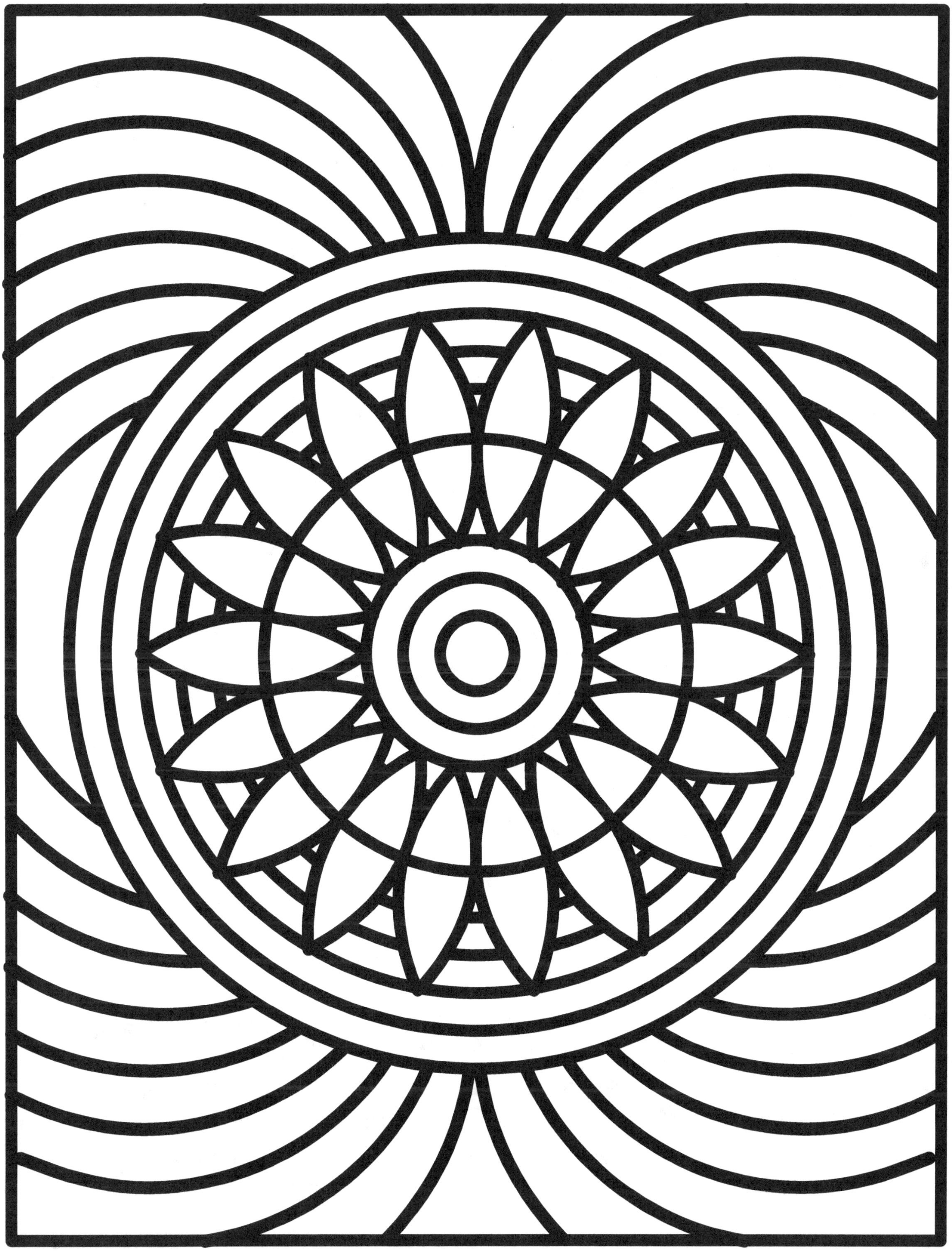

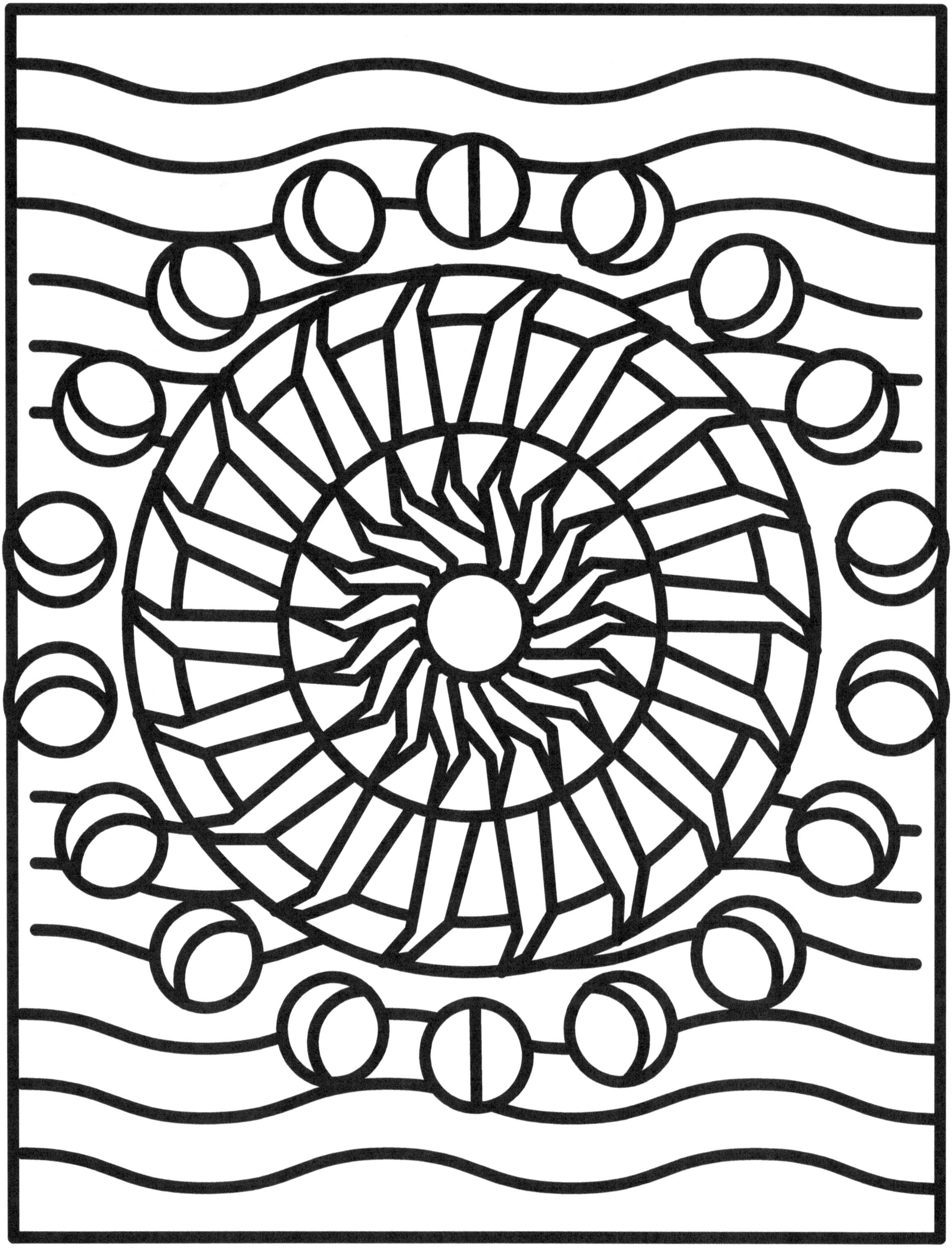

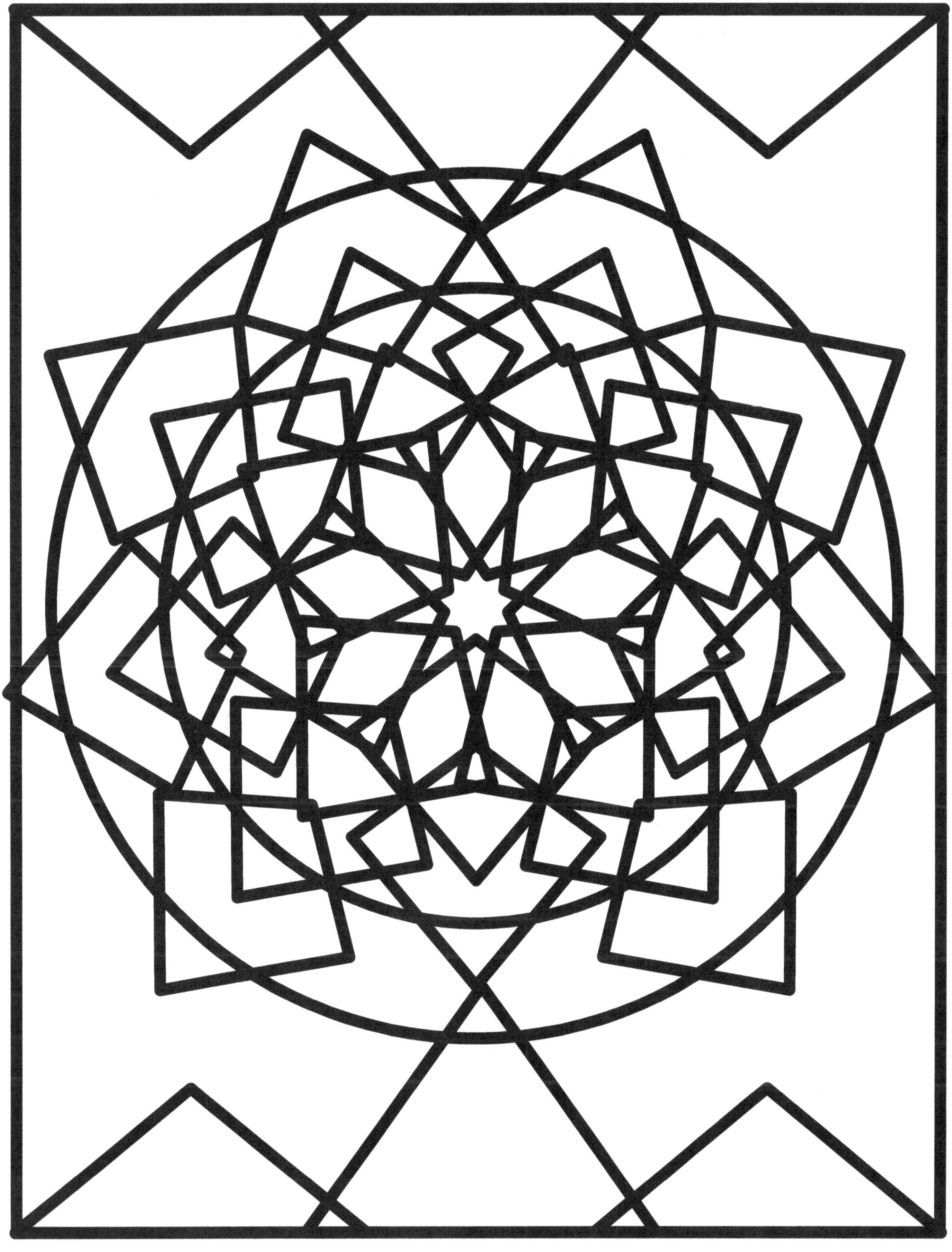

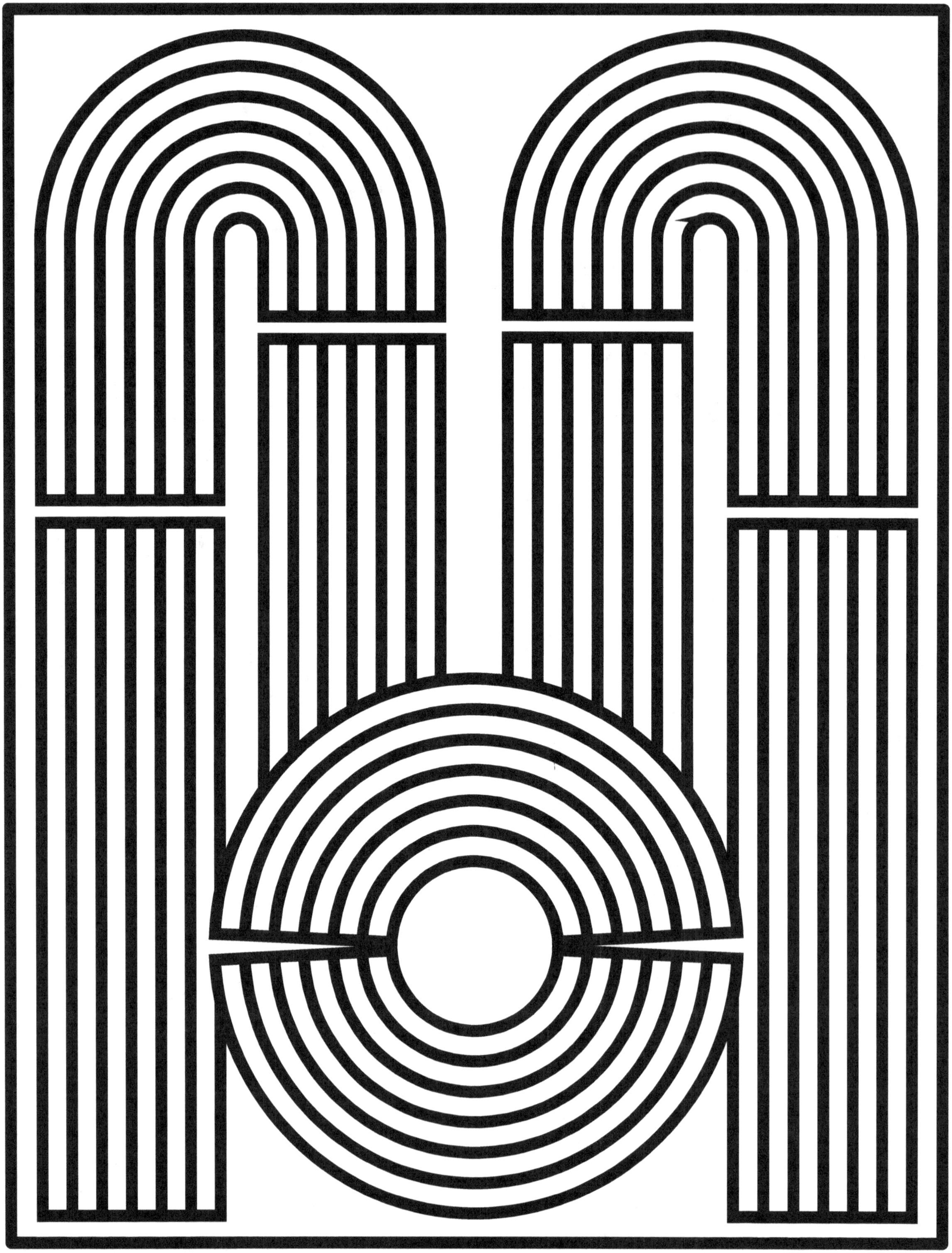

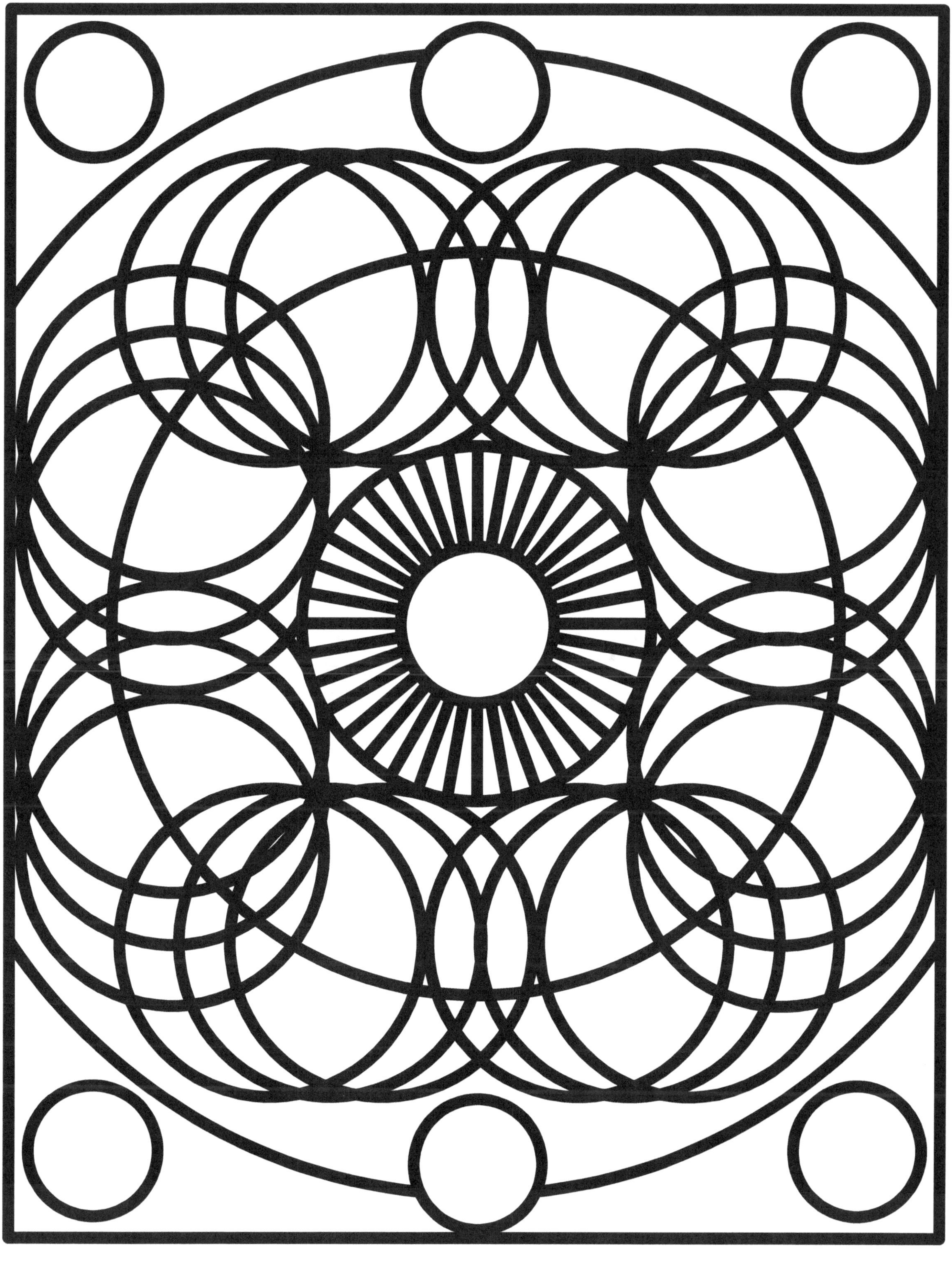

THANK YOU FOR
BEING HERE.